TRAVERSE THEATRE COMPANY
KING OF THE FIELDS
by Stuart Paterson
a new version of MR GOVERNMENT (1986)

Cast in order of appearance

Matt	Liam Brennan
Catherine	Vicki Liddelle
Willie	Russell Hunter
Tam	Robert Carr
Rab	John Kazek
Jean	Blythe Duff
Tommy	Thomas Mullins

Director	John Tiffany
Designer	Neil Warmington
Lighting Designer	Chahine Yavroyan
Composer	John Irvine
Voice/dialect Coach	Ros Steen
Assistant Director	Graeme S Maley
Stage Manager	Victoria Paulo
Deputy Stage Manager	Ella Gunn
Assistant Stage Manager	Corrie Cooper
Wardrobe Supervisor	Lynn Ferguson
Wardrobe Assistant	Caitlin Blair

First performed at the Traverse Theatre on Friday 3 December 1999

TRAVERSE THEATRE

One of the most important theatres in Britain
The Observer

Edinburgh's **Traverse Theatre** is Scotland's new writing theatre, with a 36 year record of excellence. With quality, award-winning productions and programming, the Traverse receives accolades at home and abroad from audiences and critics alike.

The Traverse has an unrivalled reputation for producing contemporary theatre of the highest quality, invention and energy, commissioning and supporting writers from Scotland and around the world and facilitating numerous script development workshops, rehearsed readings and public writing workshops. The Traverse aims to produce several major new theatre productions plus a Scottish touring production each year. It is unique in Scotland in its exclusive dedication to new writing, providing the infrastructure, professional support and expertise to ensure the development of a sustainable and relevant theatre culture for Scotland and the UK.

Traverse Theatre Company productions have been seen worldwide including London, Toronto, Budapest and New York. Recent touring successes in Scotland include HIGHLAND SHORTS (Autumn '99), PERFECT DAYS by Liz Lochhead (January - March '99) and PASSING PLACES by Stephen Greenhorn. PERFECT DAYS has recently completed a successful run at the Vaudeville Theatre in London's West End.

During the Edinburgh Festival the Traverse is one of the most important venues with award-winning, world class premieres playing daily in the two theatre spaces. In addition the Traverse presented two plays at the Edinburgh International Festival in 1999, THE MEETING by Lluïsa Cunillé and SPECULATOR by David Greig.

An essential element of the Traverse Company's activities takes place within the educational sector, concentrating on the process of playwriting for young people. The Traverse flagship education project BANK OF SCOTLAND CLASS ACT offers young people in schools the opportunity to work with theatre professionals and see their work performed on the Traverse stage. In addition the Traverse Young Writers group, led by professional playwrights, has been running for over three years and meets weekly.

STUART PATERSON

Stuart Paterson's children's plays, first performed at Glasgow's Citizens' Theatre and Edinburgh's Royal Lyceum, have been staged throughout the UK. These include MERLIN THE MAGNIFICENT, THE SNOW QUEEN, BEAUTY AND THE BEAST, CINDERELLA, GRANNY AND THE GORILLA, THE PRINCESS AND THE GOBLIN, SLEEPING BEAUTY, PETER PAN and the one-act play THE SECRET VOICE for TAG, and an adaptation of Roald Dahl's GEORGE'S MARVELLOUS MEDICINE. His recent version of HANSEL AND GRETEL for the Royal Lyceum in Edinburgh was nominated for The Barclays' Best Children's Play of the Year Award.

Stuart wrote MR GOVERNMENT in 1986 for the Royal Lyceum. KING OF THE FIELDS is a new version of this play for the Traverse Theatre.

Stuart has also written versions of Chekhov's THE CHERRY ORCHARD and UNCLE VANYA and adapted Zola's THERESE RAQUIN for Communicado Theatre Company (recently staged at Newcastle Playhouse and Edinburgh's Royal Lyceum). For Scottish Youth Theatre he has written IN TRACTION (later televised by the BBC) and adapted Zola's GERMINAL, and for the Traverse Theatre the short play THE CLEAN SWEEPS. His work for TAG includes BEOWULF, FIGHTING TALK and an adaptation of James Hogg's THE PRIVATE MEMOIRS AND CONFESSIONS OF A JUSTIFIED SINNER. He is currently working on a new version of COMRADES by August Strindberg for the Royal Lyceum.

The TV film WORKHORSES won the Pharic McLaren Award in 1985, and the short film SOMEBODY'S WEE NOBODY, directed by Gillies McKinnon, won the Gold Award at the Chicago International Film Festival. THE OLD COURSE was recently broadcast by the BBC.

Film projects include original screenplays THE PRETENDER, WHISKY MAC, UNDER THE SAME MOON, THE CHIEFTAIN'S DAUGHTER and screen adaptations of THE KELPIE'S PEARLS by Mollie Hunter, FERGUS LAMONT by Robin Jenkins and SCANDAL by Shusaku Endo.

BIOGRAPHIES

LIAM BRENNAN (Matt): For the Traverse: THE SPECULATOR (Edinburgh International Festival '99), FAMILY, KNIVES IN HENS (Edinburgh Festival Fringe '97) and WORMWOOD. His other theatre work includes seasons and productions with Dundee Rep, Perth Rep, Royal Lyceum, Sheffield Crucible, Borderline, Cumbernauld Theatre, Salisbury Playhouse, Brunton Theatre, Durham Theatre Company and Calypso Productions, Dublin. Recent theatre performances includes: Hamish in THINGS WE DO FOR LOVE (Royal Lyceum), Macbeth in MACBETH (Brunton), Edmund in KING LEAR, MER-CHANT OF VENICE (Sheffield Crucible) and Michael Collins in GOD SAVE IRELAND CRIED THE HERO (Wiseguise). Liam's television productions include: TAGGART, STRATHBLAIR, HIGH ROAD and MACHAIR and also numerous plays and short stories for BBC Radio.

ROBERT CARR (Tam): Recent theatre work includes STIFF! (Diva Productions), DEAD FUNNY, KIDNAPPED, CARLUCCO AND THE QUEEN OF HEARTS, MARY QUEEN OF SCOTS GOT HER HEAD CHOPPED OFF, TRAVESTIES, MIRANDOLINA, THE MARRIAGE OF FIGARO (Royal Lyceum), GONE FISHING, A SATIRE OF THE FOUR ESTAITES, NO EXPENSE SPARED (Wildcat), DUMBSTRUCK (Tron), THE BARBER OF SEVILLE (Arches). Film and TV includes Johnston, the Goat Farmer in MONARCH OF THE GLEN, Mad Tony in LOOKING AFTER JO JO, Mr Leitch in ORPHANS, Haldene in THE CREATIVES, THE BALDY MAN, TAGGART, Harry MacLiesh in HAMISH MACBETH and Ferret in THE HIGH LIFE.

BLYTHE DUFF (Jean): For the Traverse: The Young Playwrights' Festival, SHEILA, TALLY'S BLOOD, SHARP SHORTS. Other theatre includes over thirty productions with companies such as the Citizens' Theatre, Royal Lyceum, Cumbernauld Theatre, Wildcat, Communicado and TAG. Most recently Blythe has taken part in rehearsed readings of BLOOD RELATIVE for the Script Factory and as Masha in THREE SISTERS before an invited audience at the Haymarket Theatre, London. She has appeared in STREET SCENE playing Shirley Kaplan for Scottish Opera/English National Opera and her concert work includes BURNS BICENTENNIAL CONCERT and A YOUNG PERSON'S GUIDE TO THE ORCHESTRA for BBC Radio 3. Since 1990 Blythe has appeared as Jackie Reid in Scottish Television's TAGGART. Radio work includes THE LADY MACBETH OF MTSENSK and as a guest on JUST A MINUTE.

RUSSELL HUNTER (Willie): Now in his 53rd year in the theatre. Recent appearances for the Traverse: THE MEETING (Edinburgh International Festival '99), FAMILY, David Harrower's KILL THE OLD TORTURE THEIR YOUNG (Edinburgh Festival Fringe '98) and James Duthie's GRETA. Most recent theatre work: Andy in Brian Friel's LOVERS at the Royal Lyceum.

JOHN IRVINE (composer): KING OF THE FIELDS is John's 16th show for the Traverse. Other theatre includes KtC, Tron Theatre, Dundee Rep, Royal Lyceum, Edinburgh, Citizens Theatre, TAG, Gate Theatre, London and Lung Ha's. John works as a composer and teacher in Edinburgh and is currently co-editing an edition of *Contemporary Music Review* on Edgard Varèse with Stephen Davismoon.

JOHN KAZEK (Rab): For the Traverse: PERFECT DAYS (Traverse Festival 98, Hampstead Theatre, London and Scottish tour, Vaudeville Theatre, London), PASSING PLACES, THE CHIC NERDS, STONES AND ASHES, EUROPE. Other theatre work includes: TWELFTH NIGHT, MACBETH, A DOLL'S HOUSE (Theatre Babel); MARABOU STORK NIGHTMARES (Citizens', Leicester Haymarket); MARY QUEEN OF SCOTS GOT HER HEAD CHOPPED OFF, KIDNAPPED, CARLUCCO AND THE QUEEN OF HEARTS (Lyceum); DIAL M FOR MURDER (Dundee Rep); LOOT, DRIVING MISS DAISY, CAN'T PAY, WON'T PAY (Byre); ORPHANS (Harbinger); NAE PROBLEM, GOVAN STORIES, JUMP THE LIFE TO COME (7:84); AS YOU LIKE IT, KING LEAR (Oxford Stage Co.); GREAT EXPECTATIONS (Lyric, Belfast); JUST FRANK (Theatre Royal, Stratford East). Television and film work includes: CITY CENTRAL, RAB C NESBITT, PUNCH DRUNK, DOUBLE NOUGAT, NERVOUS ENERGY, STRATHBLAIR (BBC), TAGGART, ALBERT AND THE LION (STV); SILENT SCREAM (Antonine Productions); RIFF RAFF (Parallax Pictures).

VICKI LIDDELLE (Catherine): Trained at Queen Margaret College, Edinburgh. Theatre: THE SNOW QUEEN, BRITANNIA RULES (Royal Lyceum), THE SUICIDE, PORTRAIT OF A WOMAN (Communicado), THE GLASS MENAGERIE (Dundee Rep), MERLIN THE MAGNIFICENT, THE SNOW QUEEN (MacRobert Arts Centre), SHANGHAIED (Nippy Sweeties), PINOCCHIO (Visible Fictions), NO NEW MIRACLES (Boilerhouse), THE HAPPIEST DAYS OF YOUR LIFE (Perth Theatre), THE PRIME OF MISS JEAN BRODIE (Theatre of Comedy, London), NIGHT SKY (Stellar Quines). Film & TV: Margaret Sim in THE BIG TEASE, BBC Around Scotland Series THE SECOND WORLD WAR. Radio: MCLEVY, VIRTUAL and STILL WATERS (BBC).

GRAHAM S MALEY (assistant director): Final year Honours Student at Queen Margaret University College, Edinburgh, studying Drama and Theatre Arts and specialising in directing. Previous work includes Assistant Director for HIGHLAND SHORTS (Traverse Theatre) and workshop assistant for Borderline Theatre Company, directing Peter Handkes SELF ACCUSATION.

THOMAS MULLINS (Tommy) : Currently studying at RSAMD. His previous work includes HAMLET, GHETTO, TWELFTH NIGHT (Scottish Youth Theatre), HAVE YOU SEEN THIS GIRL (National Youth Theatre) and CINDERELLA (Scottish Ballet).

ROS STEEN (voice/dialect coach): Trained RSAMD. For the Traverse: HIGHLAND SHORTS, FAMILY, HERITAGE, KILL THE OLD TORTURE THEIR YOUNG, THE CHIC NERDS, GRETA, LAZYBED, KNIVES IN HENS, PASSING PLACES, BONDAGERS, ROAD TO NIRVANA, SHARP SHORTS, MARISOL, GRACE IN AMERICA, BROTHERS OF THUNDER. Other theatre work includes: OLEANNA, SUMMIT CONFERENCE, KRAPP'S LAST TAPE, THE DYING GAUL, CONVERSATIONS WITH A CUPBOARD MAN, EVA PERON, LONG DAY'S JOURNEY INTO NIGHT (Citizens); SEA URCHINS (Tron & Dundee Rep); A MIDSUMMER NIGHT'S DREAM (Dundee Rep); ODYSSEUS THUMP (West Yorkshire Playhouse); MYTHS OF THE NEAR FUTURE (untitled); BEUL NAM BREUG (Tosg Theatar Gaidhlig); TRAVELS WITH MY AUNT, THE PRICE (Brunton Theatre); HOME, TRANSATLANTIC, THE HANGING TREE (LookOut); TRAINSPOTTING (G & J Productions); BABYCAKES (Clyde Unity); ABIGAIL'S PARTY (Perth Rep); LOVERS, PYGMALION, OUR COUNTRY'S GOOD (Royal Lyceum); SUNSET SONG (TAG); BOLD GIRLS (Theatre Galore). Films includes: GREGORY'S TWO GIRLS, STELLA DOES TRICKS, STAND AND DELIVER. TV includes: HAMISH MACBETH, LOOKING AFTER JOJO, ST ANTHONY'S DAY OFF, CHANGING STEP.

JOHN TIFFANY (director): Trained: Glasgow University. Literary Director at the Traverse since June 1997. He directed THE JUJU GIRL, DANNY 306 + ME (4 EVER) (also Birmingham Rep), PERFECT DAYS (also Hampstead, Vaudeville and tour), GRETA, PASSING PLACES (also Citizens' and tour), SHARP SHORTS and co-directed STONES AND ASHES for the Traverse. Other theatre includes: HIDE AND SEEK and BABY, EAT UP (LookOut); THE SUNSET SHIP (Young Vic); GRIMM TALES (Leicester Haymarket); EARTHQUAKE WEATHER (Starving Artists). Film includes: KARMIC MOTHERS (BBC Tartan Shorts) and GOLDEN WEDDING (BBC Two Lives).

NEIL WARMINGTON (designer): Graduated in Fine Art at Maidstone College of Art before attending the post-graduate Theatre Design course at Motley. For the Traverse: FAMILY, PASSING PLACES (TMA Award for Best Design). Theatre credits include: RIDDANCE, CRAZYHORSE (Paines Plough); DON JUAN, TAMING OF THE SHREW (English Touring Theatre); INTIMATE EXCHANGES (Dukes Playhouse, Lancaster); LIFE IS A DREAM (TMA Award Best Design), FIDDLER ON THE ROOF (West Yorkshire Playhouse); THE DUCHESS OF MALFI (Theatre Royal, Bath); JANE EYRE (Shared Experience, Barclays Stage Award for design); WOMEN LAUGH-ING (Watford); THE TEMPEST (Contact, Manchester); DESIRE UNDER THE ELMS (Shared Experience); DISSENT, ANGELS IN AMERICA (7:84 Scot-land); TROILUS AND CRESSIDA (Opera North); HENRY V (Royal Shake-speare Company); MUCH ADO ABOUT NOTHING (Queen's Theatre, London); THE LIFE OF STUFF (Donmar Warehouse); HENRY V (RSC); WAITING FOR GODOT, MUCH ADO ABOUT NOTHING (Liverpool Everyman); COMEDIANS, ARSENIC AND OLD LACE, MERLIN (Parts 1& 2)

(Royal Lyceum); CORIOLANUS (Tramway). Neil designed the launch of Glasgow's Year of Architecture 1999, he has also won The Linbury Prize for stage design and The Sir Alfred Munnings Florence prize for painting.

CHAHINE YAVROYAN (lighting designer): Chahine trained at the Bristol Old Vic Theatre School. His previous work for the Traverse Theatre Company includes THE SPECULATOR, DANNY 306 + ME (4 EVER), PERFECT DAYS, KILL THE OLD TORTURE THEIR YOUNG, ANNA WEISS, KNIVES IN HENS, THE ARCHITECT and SHINING SOULS. He has worked extensively in theatre, with companies and artists including: Crucible, Royal Court, Lindsay Kemp, Stephen Berkoff, People Show, Leicester Haymarket, ICA, Hackney Empire, Hampstead, Manchester Royal Exchange, Nottingham Playhouse and Bush Theatres. Dance work includes: Yolande Snaith Theatredance, Bock & Vincenzi, Anatomy Performance Company, The Place, Haughmond Abbey and the Purcell Rooms. Chahine has also worked on many site specific works including various events and celebrations for the city of Bologna, Italy. He is a long-standing People Show person.

KING OF THE FIELDS
Set, props and costumes by the Traverse Workshops
Funded by The Scottish Arts Council National Lottery Fund

For KING OF THE FIELDS:

Production Photography   Kevin Low

Print Photography   Euan Myles

Wardrobe Care   **LEVER BROTHERS**

Audio Description - Sunday December 12 - provided by the Audio Description Association (Scotland)
BSL Sign Language Interpretation - Sunday December 12 - provided by Lisa Stapleton from the Edinburgh and East of Scotland Deaf Society.

TRAVERSE THEATRE - THE COMPANY

KING OF THE FIELDS

Stuart Paterson

Characters

CATHERINE REID
MATTHEW REID
WILLIE COLE
TAM BURNET
ROBERT REID
JEAN CAIRNEY
TOMMY CAIRNEY

Setting: Ayrshire, 1935.

King of the Fields is a revised and rewritten version of *Mister Government*, first performed at the Royal Lyceum Theatre, Edinburgh, in 1986.

Songs

'Oh, love, love, love . . . ' is from 'Love is Like a Dizziness' (James Hogg, 1770–1835).

'Come ill or well, the cross, the crown . . . ' is from 'Youth And Love' (Robert Louis Stevenson, 1850–1894).

'An' this shall be for music . . . ' is from 'I Will Make You Brooches' (Robert Louis Stevenson).

'I wid hae gi'en him my lips tae kiss . . . .' is from 'Mary's Song' (Marion Angus, 1886–1946).

'There was a sang . . . .' is from 'There Was A Sang' (Helen Cruickshank, 1886–1975).

Act One

Stage in darkness. The sound of brisk steps and a light is snapped on. A small, sparsely furnished bedroom.
CATHERINE REID *has entered, and stands by the bed, holding a bundle of sheets and blankets. She is a pretty, vital girl of nineteen.*

MATT REID, *a strongly-built man in his late thirties, sits half up in the bed, his head slumped forward.*

CATHERINE. Are you awake? I know you're awake . . . Wake up . . . (*He lifts his head and stares at* CATHERINE *in confusion.*) You'll need to get up . . . I'm going to change the sheets . . . Do you hear me? You'll need to get up. (MATT *rises unsteadily from the bed. His pyjama trousers are wet.* CATHERINE *strips the bed, hands* MATT *a clean pair of pyjamas.*) You'll want these . . . (*He steps out of his pyjamas and stands in a daze.* CATHERINE *makes up the bed.*) I looked in on you a short while ago . . . Your eyes were wide open . . . Thought you were dead . . . Thought I was looking at a corpse . . . Then I saw the blankets moving when you breathed . . . (*He slowly puts on his clean pyjamas, begins to sing quietly.*)

MATT. Oh, love, love, love!
Love is like a dizziness;
It wilnae let a pair body
Gang about his biziness!

CATHERINE. That's the way . . . Have a sing . . . (*He sings more loudly, defiantly.*)

MATT. Come ill or well, the cross, the crown,
The rainbow or the thunder,
I fling my soul and body down
For God to plough them under.

He hangs his head, exhausted.

CATHERINE. What's wrong? Have I made you ashamed?
I didn't mean to . . . Get back into bed . . . (*He sits on the*

bed.) That's a good . . . That's good. (*He lies back and she pulls the blankets up over him.*) What's wrong? Tell me . . . (*He looks up at her.*) Tell me. (*He turns away, and she gathers up the sheets, goes to the door and puts out the light.*)

MATT. No! (*She puts the light back on.*)

CATHERINE. Is it the dark? I could leave the light on . . . I often sleep with the light on . . . It's no' so quiet then . . . Or I could sit by you . . . Would you like that? You should sleep, but I'll sit by you if you like . . . (*She sits at the end of the bed.*) You'll be comfier now . . . You'll can sleep . . . It's that quiet out here in the country sometimes you think the whole world is dead . . . It gets that dark it's like a cave . . . Say if you want me to go . . . Just say . . . I'm from the city . . . You can always hear a noise there when you want . . Maybe you're the bear . . . The bear in the cave . . . Are you the bear? . . . (*She is embarrassed.*) Stupid . . . I'll go . . . You'll be alright now . . . I'll go . . . (*She moves to the door.*)

MATT. There's nothing the matter! Nothing! Do you hear me?

CATHERINE. I hear you.

MATT. I woke up in the dark . . . I didnae ken whaur . . . Whaur I'd come tae . . .

CATHERINE. You're fine now.

MATT. Can you no' hear me? There's nothin' wrang wi' me . . . They couldnae dae without me . . . When the big gun got stuck in the mire they'd ca' for me by name . . . By name! And me and the horse would pull it clear th'gither . . . We'd soon get things movin' again . . . I ken how tae work a horse . . . They'd ca' for me by name . . . (*He hangs his head.* CATHERINE *sits on the end of the bed.*) It was dark, that's all there is about it . . .

CATHERINE. You're home now.

MATT. Hame?

CATHERINE. Willie Cole found you when he was locking up . . . Behind the oil drums in Rab's yard . . . Willy thought

you were a tramp but I knew you from the photos . . .
Matthew Reid . . . Don't know how we got you to the
house . . .

MATT. Rab . . . Rab's still here richt enough?

CATHERINE. This is his house . . .

MATT. He could hae gone anywhere . . . He could hae been
lost to me.

CATHERINE. He's away working . . . Away for a load . . .

MATT. Wha does he work for?

CATHERINE. Himsel'.

MATT. Himsel'?

CATHERINE. Ain truck, yard wi' a petrol pump, workshop . . .

MATT. A businessman . . . It's no' easy done that . . .

CATHERINE. He's ay working . . . You cannae stop him . . .

MATT. A businessman, by Christ . . . You his lassie?

CATHERINE. Aye?

MATT. Where's your mother?

CATHERINE. My mother? How? (*Understands.*) Wife . . . I'm
his wife, no' his lassie . . .

MATT. How old are you?

CATHERINE. Nineteen.

MATT. Gey young.

CATHERINE. Ken . . . You're thirty-nine.

MATT. How would you ken?

CATHERINE. Rab talks about you a' the time . . . We got
married on your birthday . . . I'm Catherine . . .

MATT. He hasnae forgot his brother?

CATHERINE. No fear . . . Thirty-nine, eh?

MATT. Forty near.

CATHERINE. Gey auld.

MATT. Gey auld.

CATHERINE. He'll be that pleased to see you . . . It'll lift him up . . . He's needin' that . . . He'll no' know what to do wi' himsel', he'll be that delighted . . . I'm pleased too . . .

MATT. What are you pleased for?

CATHERINE (*shrugs*). I'm no' well liked here . . . (*Fixes blankets.*)

MATT (*with sudden fierceness*). I'm no' needin' lookin' after! There's nothin' wrang wi' me! A man loses his strength, that's a' . . . It soon comes back . . . (*More gently.*) How are you no' well liked?

CATHERINE. You should sleep.

MATT. How are you no' well liked here?

CATHERINE. I'm from the city . . . An incomer they cry me . . . They smile right enough, them that ken how, but I'm no' so stupid I cannae tell by the way they look at me I'm no' well liked . . . I cannae do a' they do . . . Bakin', knittin', twistin the neck o' a hen till it's deid . . . You should see them . . . Spend a' day in front o' the oven shovellin' it full o' a' kinds o' things you wouldnae believe, like they're runnin' a train no' a house . . . I'm lost when it comes to a' they things . . . They like to see me lost, so they do . . . They think I'm Rab's ruin . . . Sometimes, I shouldnae say this, but there are days when I'm walkin' past them I walk a' confident and strong so's to make them think we dae it different in the city . . . Head up, no' lookin' to right or left . . . Aye but I see them lookin', turnin' their heads, a' the men . . . (*Drops her head.*) Maybe they don't . . .

MATT. Aye they look . . . Rab'll like that . . . A' the men lookin' . . .

CATHERINE. He doesnae see they things . . .

MATT. He's done well, then . . . He's done well for himsel' . . .

CATHERINE. Aye.

MATT. So have you, Christ! Ain house, time on your hands, married to my brother . . . I hope you're no' one o' they lassies that's just tak, tak, tak . . . I hope for Rab's sake you're no' one o' them.

CATHERINE. You should sleep.

MATT. I'm no' ready for sleep . . . Tell me how you pass the time here in my hame, here at the place of my birth . . .

CATHERINE. I'm no' idle . . . Keepin' this house . . . Whiles I help Rab wi' the accounts . . . I take him a meal if he's busy in the office . . . Answer the phone . . . When the phone rings it's like he's seen his ain ghost . . . He hates talkin' on the phone . . .

MATT. That's no' a guid thing that, in a businessman . . . Likely soon you'll hae bairns . . .

CATHERINE. Likely . . . How have you passed all this time you've been away? (*No response.*) How have you passed the time?

MATT. There's mony a concern made guid use o' me! Folk tak one look at me an' mark me down as a man wha can be trusted . . . I've ay found myself a position . . . The minute I walk into a firm I'm noticed . . . People can sense a big hert in a man . . . It gies them strength, aye, an' hope alang wi' it . . . I've kent some boys wha've lost their hert, put it away somewhere safe till it cannae be found again when it's wanted . . . But no' me . . . No sir, no' me . . . Are you there, are you listenin'?

CATHERINE. I'm here.

MATT. The time's no' passed me by! On the move a' my life . . . You cannae stay in the yin place . . . They'll tak you for granted, forget your name, ca' you by another boy's name . . . A man learns to tak what he wants . . . If it's no' there he looks till he finds it . . . They called for me by name . . . The officers . . . Couldnae dae without me . . . (*He tires and fades.*) A man loses his strength . . . It soon comes back . . .

He lies back, closes his eyes. CATHERINE *pulls up the blankets. Loud shouts from outside. She moves to the door, puts out the light.*

Lights up on kitchen. An armchair, table and chairs, a stove and sink. The room is dominated by an old clock which has no clockface, only a faint glow of light.

Enter WILLIE COLE *and* TAM BURNET. WILLIE *is a
small, quick man of sixty or so.* TAM *is a big, decent man
in his fifties. They wear tattered oil-blackened overalls.*
WILLIE, *already a little the worse for drink, treasures a
half-bottle.*

WILLIE. Matt, Mattie-boy, Matthew Reid . . . Come on here
till we mak' you welcome . . .

TAM. Haud your wheesht, Willie . . . Onybody would think
you were in your ain house, so they would, so they would . . .

WILLIE. Away! I'm doin' fine . . . (*Enter* CATHERINE.)
Mistress Reid . . . (*Bows.*) The woman o' my dreams . . .

CATHERINE. You're fu' again, Willie Cole.

WILLIE. I'm no' fu', I'm cheery, there's a wide difference . . .
Are they a' like you in the city?

TAM. Dinnae pay him ony heed, Mistress Reid . . . Come awa
hame, Willie . . .

WILLIE. I'm here to see Matt Reid . . . Hell o' a state for a
man like that to come hame . . . A tramp just . . . But we'll
hae flags an' fireworks just the same . . .

CATHERINE. It's late . . . Come tomorrow . . .

TAM. Come on, Willie, leave it the now . . .

WILLIE. The return hame o' a trueborn son o' th'Ayrshire soil!
If a man cannae celebrate that there's nae joy left in the
world . . . Nane at a' . . .

TAM (*leading* WILLIE *firmly by the arm*). Goodnight to you,
Mistress Reid . . .

WILLIE (*pulling free*). Awa' tae hell! I'm here to see Matt
Reid and Matt Reid's the man I'll see!

Enter MATT. *He wears a dark, ragged greatcoat. He seems
lost, uncertain.* TAM *is shocked by the change in* MATT.

WILLIE. There, you see . . . What did I tell you? The man
himsel' . . .

CATHERINE. You're up, Matt.

*He seems not to have heard. He looks warily around the
room, at* CATHERINE, *then down, defeated at his feet.*

WILLIE (*trying as best he can to dispel the awkwardness*).
I ken the feelin' fine, Matt son . . . You're up, but you
dinnae ken if you're dancin' . . . Come on ower here . . .
Ower here where it's warm . . . (*He pulls out a chair.*) On
you come . . .

MATT. I'm no' needin' the help o' any man!

WILLIE. Just as you say, Matt, just as you say . . .

MATT *sits slowly and unsteadily in the chair.*

CATHERINE. I'll get you something to eat.

MATT. I'm no' needin' to eat . . . I'm past eatin' . . . Thank-
you.

WILLIE. Aye, but you'll hae a drink . . . Here . . . (MATT
takes the bottle and drinks.) Do you no' ken me, Matt?

MATT. I heard voices . . . I thought Rab was here . . . I thocht
maybe the businessman was hame . . .

CATHERINE. He had a load up north . . . He shouldnae be
long now . . .

WILLIE. Do you no' ken me?

MATT. I'll ken my brother when I see him . . . I'll no' mistake
him . . . It'll be guid to see my brother . . .

WILLIE. Nae doubt, but you've friends here the noo' come to
welcome you hame . . . Come to talk wi' you and mak you
cheery . . . Aye, aye . . . You'll ken your faither's deid?

TAM. Willie!

WILLIE. Naw, naw, I'm no' so daft . . . These things have to
be said . . . He could be sittin' there no' wantin' to ask,
hopin' for a sicht o' his faither . . .

MATT. I didnae ken, but I thocht it likely . . .

WILLIE. Whaur hae you been, Matt? I counted out the year . . .
Sixteen year . . . Whaur hae you been for sixteen year?

TAM (*trying to spare* MATT *from having to answer*). You're
hame noo'.

MATT. I could eat . . . I think I could eat . . .

WILLIE. Do you no' ken me? Willie Cole . . . You must ken
auld King Cole . . .

MATT. I ken you fine, Willie.

WILLIE (*hurt*). I didnae think you could forget . . . (*Indicates* TAM.) An' him? Do you no' ken him?

MATT (*looking closely at* TAM). Geordie . . . Geordie Burnet . . . (CATHERINE *places some food in front of* MATT.)

TAM. Warm.

WILLIE. No' Geordie . . . Geordie's deid . . . Geordie's son . . .

MATT. His son?

TAM *lifts his old cap, reveals his bald head or white hair.*

TAM. That's my faither, so it is, so it is . . .

WILLIE. Is he no' the very image o' auld Geordie?

MATT (*shocked into laughter*). The very image . . . Can a man no' hae ony dignity in this God-forsaken country?

WILLIE. Life goes on its way and it doesnae pay ony heed to dignity or its cousins . . .

MATT. It's good to see you, Tam . . . (*Shakes his hand.*)

TAM. Welcome hame . . . Welcome hame . . .

MATT. I'll drink to that . . .

CATHERINE (*Takes the bottle*). No you'll no' . . . You'll eat first . . . Go on.

MATT. It seems I've to eat . . . Right then, I'll eat . . . (*He eats.*)

WILLIE. So there you are . . . Even as a boy you had a way o' bringin' things to life . . . You've been sairly missed . . .

MATT. Not at a' . . .

WILLIE. Just seein' you sit there an' it's no' the back o' beyond ony mair . . . A' o' a sudden it's the place to be . . . You ay had a way wi' you . . .

TAM. Mind yon big horse o' Cuthbert's . . .

WILLIE. Big Blackie.

TAM. Aye, Blackie.

MATT. I mind it.

TAM. Naebody could mak it dae a minute's work but wi' you it was that strong an' willin' we'd be feart it might pull the earth aff its turn . . .

WILLIE. A' it needed was a guid man to keep it richt . . .

MATT. I could ay work a horse . . . I mind that well . . .

TAM. You've a need to mind they things . . .

WILLIE. Aye, but it's a' tractors noo' . . . An' we work for Rab.

MATT. You're Rab's men?

WILLIE. Cuthbert threw us aff his farm . . .

TAM. His two boys grew up . . . Took our places . . .

WILLIE. I mind the pumps, dae some drivin', Tam sees to the workshop side o' things . . . It's gey often the busiest part . . .

TAM. It's a' they buggert tractors . . .

WILLIE. If it wasnae for Rab startin' up on his ain, we'd be finished, starvin' in the road like a' they other boys you read about in the paper . . . Mind you, an' nae offence tae Rab, but if I ever thocht I'd finish up workin' for a Reid, I'd hae put money on it bein' you, Matt . . . Guid money . . .

TAM. No' that Rab hasnae done well . . .

WILLIE. Oh, aye, he's done well . . . You can see that . . . A' you need dae is look at his wife . . .

CATHERINE. Willie Cole!

WILLIE (*to* MATT). If a young lassie cannae tak' a compliment . . .

CATHERINE. Sometimes the way you speak I need to look down to check I'm in the room wi' you . . . It's no' good manners.

WILLIE. Aye, she'll be missin' the city . . .

CATHERINE (*calling off*). Are you there, Catherine? Are you there? Come away through, there's a man here talkin' to you . . . (*To* WILLIE.) Aye, there's time when I miss the city . . .

WILLIE. That's what I said.

CATHERINE. God save us.

MATT. I ken a' the cities o' England . . . It's no' the city that's worth a damn, it's the city that lies inside a man . . . Some men hae a' the lang streets, bricht lichts an' dances that ony lassie could wish for . . .

WILLIE (*stirred*). That's it, Matt son! The city that lies inside a man . . . That's just the way o' it! An' that's the Matt Reid I mind! You had a magic tae you . . . If your faither could hae been here . . . When a man comes hame frae a war he wants to come hame a champion . . . He doesnae want to come hame wi' nothin' to his name . . . (*Tearful.*) That's why I wanted to talk wi' you . . . For your faither's sake . . . You had a great strength . . .

MATT. Aye-aye . . .

TAM (*firmly*). Hame, Willie.

WILLIE. Let me finish! (*Recovers himself.*) You're the last yin hame an' nane the worse for that . . . You've it a' in front o' you . . . Just mind this, you'll ay be a champion to your ain folk . . .

TAM. Hame!

WILLIE. A bloody champion . . .

The sound of a truck engine.

MATT. Rab . . .

CATHERINE. That's him . . .

MATT. My boots! I'll need my boots . . . Where are my boots?

CATHERINE (*smiling, taking his arm gently*). Never mind your boots . . . You're fine the way you are . . .

RAB *crosses the dimly lit yard outside. He is a wiry, good-looking man of thirty-two. He stops as if he senses something, and enters, but does not immediately see* MATT. CATHERINE *goes to him.*

RAB (*tired*). How's my wee bobbydazzler? (*She smiles and steps aside.*) Matthew? Is it? Matt . . .

MATT. Rab.

RAB (*quietly*). I cannae find the words . . .

MATT. We're no' needin' ony words . . .

They embrace.

TAM. Come on, an' gie folk their privacy.

WILLIE. Flags an' fireworks . . .

TAM (*takes* WILLIE *firmly by the arm*). Bricht an' early the morn, Rab . . . Goodnicht, yin an' a' . . . (*He leads* WILLIE *out.*)

RAB. I never thocht the day would come . . . God knows I've wished for it often enough . . . Sit down, sit down . . . You're hame . . . Just sayin' it's a pleasure . . .

CATHERINE (*to* RAB.) You'll be hungry . . .

RAB. I'm no' needin' onythin' . . . You're hame, Matt . . .

CATHERINE. I've it ready . . .

RAB. Don't fuss! But Matt, have you seen tae him? (*To* MATT.) She's just a young lassie . . .

MATT. She's done me proud.

CATHERINE. I'll go to bed.

RAB. She's a guid lassie . . .

CATHERINE. You'll want to talk . . . (*She goes.*)

MATT. A fine lassie.

RAB. I'd be lost wi'out her.

MATT. You've done well . . . I've been hearin' . . . A business-man, by Christ . . .

RAB. Aye, I am that.

MATT. Robert Reid . . . I've ay minded you as a boy, skin an' bone just . . . Faither would hae been that proud . . . (RAB *looks up quickly.*) You're a' richt, son . . . Willie Cole tellt me . . .

RAB. It was six year ago . . . Illness had him walk wi' a stoop as if he couldnae wait for the earth to claim him . . . No' that he'd stop his work, you ken what he was like . . . Yon tyrant Grier worked him to the grave . . . But he never stopped talkin' about you . . . "Matt'll ken what he's after," that's what he'd say . . . "Matt'll show us a' the way." He'd

never a doubt in his heid you were livin' . . . An' the things
he had you daein' . . . Drivin' your ain motor, flyin' across
the Rockies . . . Runnin' the hale country damned near . . .

MATT. It's as well I bided awa'.

RAB. How's that?

MATT. Look at me.

RAB. I see you fine.

MATT. Look at me! I'm no' what I was . . .

RAB. You are to me . . .

MATT. Then you're blin'.

RAB. You've ay been a man to me, Matt . . . Best there ever
was . . . You've no' changed . . . Faither was proud o' you . . .

MATT. A weak man wants his sons to be strong.

RAB. He was never weak, Matt.

MATT. He was big, an' he could be hard when he wanted, but
he was never strong . . . Aye, he could talk . . . What a' he
wasnae goin' t'dae . . . Died a peasant like I ay ways kent he
would . . . A beast in a stinkin' field . . . So here's tae
Robert Reid, his ain man in his ain hoose . . . Christ, have
you no' got a bottle? What kin o' hoose doesnae hae a bottle
at the ready? Is it a church you've built?

RAB. Aye, I've a bottle . . . (*Pours whisky, hands one to*
MATT.)

MATT. Here's to my brother, the boy, and the man.

RAB. To my brother . . . (*The clock chimes the half hour.*) I've
needed you . . . I've needed you that much . . .

MATT. I've travelled that far . . . I'm here now . . . I'm
standin' here . . .

RAB. Will you bide hame, Matt?

MATT. We'll need to see . . .

RAB. There's a hame here if you want it.

MATT. I've interests . . . Interests that need my best attention . . .
A man cannae go for sixteen year wi'out gatherin' up his share
o' responsibilities . . . Here an' there . . . Bits an' pieces . . .

You'll ken a' aboot that, bein' a man o' business . . . You need to keep a watch on your affairs, or they'll slip awa' . . . Slip back . . .

RAB. Bide hame.

MATT. We'll need to see . . . (*Pours drinks.*) Mair drink an' enough o' Matt Reid . . . How did you manage it, a' this . . . Dinnae tell me you won it at cards.

RAB. Worked a' the hours God gave me . . . Drove a bus, Glasgow an' back twice a day for eight year . . . Watched them build the new road, listened to the other drivers, no' just the bus boys . . . The hale world was movin' on the roads . . . Bein' your ain man wasnae just a dream ony mair . . . Easy to say, I ken, but it came to hae a meanin' for me . . . I started to believe it . . . Went to the bank wi' the money I'd put by . . . You should hae seen me, Matt . . . When I stepped into the office I was shakin' like I had the fever . . . What richt had I tae be my ain man? Everythin' came out arse about . . . But the bank boy, he wasnae a bad boy, he tellt me to slow down an', by Christ, if he didnae finish up by throwin' money at me . . .

MATT. He would hae seen you were a guid man.

RAB. He could see that wi' the new road an' the fair price o' land there was mair than a notion here, there was money to be made . . .

MATT. An' that was you on the way up . . .

RAB. Bocht my waggon, took on Tam an' Willie, built this house when I wasnae workin' . . .

MATT. And then you brocht a woman hame to the house you'd built.

RAB. She . . . Catherine . . . She worked in the canteen at the docks . . . A' the boys had a notion for her . . . I'd go in even if I didnae hae a load . . . Just to look at her . . . Just to look at her walk across the flair . . .

MATT. The empire o' a guid man . . . You've it a', Rab . . .

RAB. Aye, you'd think it, I ken . . . It can be gey lonely bein' your ain man . . .

MATT. Away! Lonely? Not at a' . . . (*Picks up bottle.*) You'll hae another . . .

RAB. No' for me, Matt.

MATT. Aye you will . . . (*Pours drinks.*) Come on an' we'll get the birch th'gither . . . (*They drink.*) You'll be up the front o' the kirk noo' . . .

RAB (*laughs*). Aye . . .

MATT. You're a richt dignitary gettin' . . .

RAB. Ken . . . Whiles I go shootin' wi' the fermers an' their pals . . . It's no' a safe occupation, I'm tellin' you . . . An' at Christmas there I was invited t'partake in Major Telford's curlin' match . . . Out on the ice wi' a' the kiltie-bums wi' their siller flasks, aye, wi' initials on them tae, as if the drink had been made just for the like o' they . . .

MATT. Not at a' . . . You're best to keep in wi' folk like they . . .

RAB. Aye . . . A' this here, it's been my dream, what other dream is there? . . . But there's times when I think I'll lose it a' . . . It's taken that much to get this far . . .

MATT. That's no guid talk . . .

RAB. There's nothing means mair tae me than havin' nae bugger t'tell me what an' what no' t'dae . . . But dreams weigh heavy, Matt, they're no just wee puffs o' air . . . There's times when I'm feart I cannae keep haud o' it . . . I'm a worker . . . I need tae think to write my name . . . How've I the right tae be my ain man?

MATT. Weakness.

RAB. No, listen . . .

MATT. No, I'll no' bloody listen . . . Lonely, feart, dreams . . . What kind o' words are they? You've come up frae nothin', an' you've every right tae believe in yoursel' . . . An' if you cannae . . . The world is full o' meanness an' filth . . . If you cannae believe . . . They'll throw you on a dung-hill an' heap rubbish on tap o' you till you cannae breathe . . . (*Struggles for breath.*)

RAB. What's wrang, Matt?

MATT. You're as guid as ony man! Awa' wi' you!

RAB. What is it?

MATT. There's nothin' wrang wi' me, Christ . . . I've been
ill . . . I've had an illness . . .

RAB. An illness?

MATT. Had mind, no' hae, but it's held me back, lost me
time . . . When I was fighting for my country I was
poisoned wi' the gas, no' just the once, an' the pain o' it,
Christ . . . Went to this doctor an' he says to me – once yon
muck gets down deep it's there for guid, it'll never leave
you . . . As if I couldnae hae tellt him that mysel' . . . He
said I didnae hae long . . .

RAB. Matt . . .

MATT. Dinnae whine at me! It was four year ago I saw the
doctor . . . Four year . . . If that's no' long I'd like tae ken
what is . . . Gas, disease . . . What kind o' words are they?
A man can beat they things if he musters his strength alang
wi' his will . . . I've beat it, I'm tellin' you . . . I've beat it . . .

RAB. I believe you, Matt . . .

MATT. An' why should you no'? I could break you in half . . .
I'm as strong as ever I was . . . Four year . . . (MATT *stands
looking at the clock.*) I mind a boy wha shared an attic room
wi' me . . . I says tae him afore I moved in – a' right is it,
this room? You can live in it, he says, but the funny thing
about attics, like pubs an' picture-houses, he says – they mak
you lose a' sense o' time . . . An' like a clown I ask him –
how long have you stayed here? Now how would I ken that,
he says . . . How would I ken that?

RAB. I've wanted you hame . . . A partner, my brother . . . I
believe you, Matt . . .

MATT. This clock . . . It belongs tae me, does it no'?

RAB. It was our faither's, an' his faither's afore that . . . Had
ay tae go tae the eldest son . . . It's yours, Matt . . .

MATT. A belonging . . . Something that belonged to me afore I
was born . . .

RAB. You ken what I mind, Matt . . . I mind when you used to
sit me on the plough . . . You said it was to gie it wecht, to
help it cut deep, but that was just kindness . . . It seems to
me I've been there a' my life . . . Between you an' the
horse, the sky an' the earth, movin' slow, you a man an' me
a boy, me a boy an' you a man . . . It seems I've been there
a' my life . . .

The clock slowly strikes midnight. MATT *moves slowly to
where* RAB *is sitting, stands tall above him.*

MATT. I've travelled that far . . . I'm here now . . . I'm
standin' here . . .

Fade lights.

Act Two

*Day. The kitchen, and the yard outside – a small hut/office,
mounds of tyres, scattered oil drums and discarded engine
parts. A telephone wire, attached to the wall of the hut, recedes
into the bright, cold distance of the open countryside.*

CATHERINE *sits alone in the kitchen. She knits clumsily, with
great concentration. Losing patience, she puts the knitting
down, stands and takes a packet of cigarettes from a secret
place. She lights one, plays at smoking like a film-star.*

MATT *comes out of the yard office. He still wears the
greatcoat, but looks stronger now. He crosses the yard and
enters the kitchen, unseen by* CATHERINE. *He admires her,
then knocks quietly, causing her to start with fright.*

CATHERINE (*recovering herself*). I thought you were Rab . . .
He doesnae like me to smoke . . . He doesnae think it looks
guid in a lassie.

MATT. Nae harm in a secret.

CATHERINE (*putting out her cigarette*). You were early up
again . . .

MATT. Did I wake you?

CATHERINE. I was lyin' awake.

MATT. There's nae guid in that.

CATHERINE. Rab can sleep . . . He's like a bairn . . .

MATT. Rab's a guid man.

CATHERINE (*returning to her knitting*). Where do you find to go so early?

MATT. Tap o' the hill at the back o' Pollock's farm . . . It's fine and clear up there in the morning . . . As if you could start your life ower again . . . (*He touches a ball of wool.*) You're fair hammerin' alang wi' the wool.

CATHERINE (*laughing*). I'll get quicker . . .

MATT. Aye, but would you want to?

CATHERINE. I wouldnae want to get any slower.

MATT (*playing with the wool*). Up on Pollock's hill . . . Walkin' the old walks . . . There's a glow to the world . . . The water . . . It tastes o' sky . . . Mind how I tellt you it was like on the road when you've left it a' behind . . .

CATHERINE. And you've nae idea what's in front o' you . . . Aye, I mind . . .

MATT. It's like that, but you're hame . . . (*He slowly unravels her knitting.*) There's times up there when I can see a' there is to see, an' whiles when I touch a thing I can feel inside what maks it work . . . (*Sings quietly as he unravels her wool.*)

An' this shall be for music when naeb'dy else is near,
The fine song for singin', the rare song tae hear!
That only I remember, that only you admire,
O' the broad road that stretches and the roadside fire.

CATHERINE (*surprised into laughter*). What are you doin'? Stop it . . .

MATT. I'm stronger now . . .

CATHERINE (*angered*). I said stop it! (*He leaves go of the wool.*) You've nae right t'dae that.

MATT. We can talk . . . I tell you stories . . . I ken you like that . . .

CATHERINE. What do you think I am? Some wee lassie.
(*Lights a cigarette.*)

MATT. I'm no' used wi' folk . . . I'm no' used wi' houses . . .

CATHERINE. I'm no' easy . . .

RAB (*from off*). Matt? Matt, is that you? (CATHERINE *starts
guiltily.* MATT *takes the cigarette from her, smokes it. Enter
RAB carrying an accounts ledger.*) You're there, Matt. I've
been doin' the books . . . A' bloody mornin' . . . (*Sits at the
table, his back to* MATT.) See columns o' figures, they're
no' half the job for makin' a man feel sma' . . . I sit lookin'
at them . . . (CATHERINE *kisses his head, gently strokes
his neck.*) One minute I see it clear as day, an' the next I
cannae see a way forrit at a' an' I'm the bank's man the rest
o' my days . . . (CATHERINE *continues to stroke his neck.*)
You're my wee bobbydazzler . . . But I like t'think o' you
in the office, Matt. It feels that right to me . . . (*Laughs.*)
An' you should hear him on the phone . . . He was on tae
Ferguson's for they engine parts that're weeks late . . .
(*Closes his eyes, smiles.*) Dinnae blether on tae me about
business, Matt tells him, or I'll come through the phone to
you an' buy your stinkin' business . . . (MATT *leaves
silently, stands in the yard smoking the cigarette.*) We'll get
the parts noo', I says to mysel' . . . Aye, you're no' feart,
Matt, an' you've big ideas . . . That's the best o' it . . .
(MATT *goes into the office.*) Have you heard ony mair
about the London load? That's where the big money is, you're
richt . . . Long distance . . . Have you heard onythin' back?

CATHERINE (*gently*). He's away back out, Rab . . .

RAB. He's no' here? Aye well, he'll likely be back at his
desk . . . I've dreamed o' it bein' like this . . . A' my life . . .
Can you see the difference in him? He's a new man . . .

CATHERINE. There's pain in him yet.

RAB. Naw, naw, a' they years, the illness, that's a' deid an'
gone . . . He's hame noo' . . .

CATHERINE. You give him too much.

RAB. An' what would you ken about it?

CATHERINE. I'm no' blind.

RAB. You're a young lassie just.

CATHERINE. I'm your wife.

RAB. You're my wee bobbydazzler, you ken that.

CATHERINE. I'm Catherine . . . Catherine!

RAB. This is no' like you . . .

CATHERINE. I want to talk, that's a'.

RAB. What's there to talk about?

CATHERINE. Last night . . . Do you no' mind?

RAB. I mind it fine.

CATHERINE. Tell me what you mind . . . Tell me.

RAB. It wasnae cold, but you'd lit a fire . . . There were shadows on the ceilin' frae the flames . . . Shapes dancin' on the wall by the bed . . . You were that lovely . . .

CATHERINE. You talked an' talked . . .

RAB. I had things clear . . . Matt an' me th'gither . . . For once I had things clear . . .

CATHERINE. You left me alone.

RAB. I was there by you . . . You werenae alone . . .

CATHERINE. When you brought me here you promised to help me make a home . . .

RAB. This is our hame, an' a damned fine yin at that!

CATHERINE. I'll go off my head . . . You were the kindest, maist gentle man I'd ever met . . . But livin' here, in this place . . . Wi' nothin' but fields an' fields . . . An' the people . . . Christ, the people . . .

RAB. It'll tak' time . . .

CATHERINE. The other morning in the village I heard the women talkin' . . . Imagine Bobby Reid waitin' a' this time just t'marry a doll . . . A doll . . .

RAB. So that's what they're sayin'?

CATHERINE (*astonished*). You believe them? You do . . . I can see it . . .

RAB. Naw, naw . . . Come here, come here close, that's the way . . . (*Pulls her close.*) Some things are best no' said . . . They're best kept quiet till another day comes round an' maybe then they're no' needin' said nae mair . . .

CATHERINE. I could scream . . .

RAB (*suddenly erupting in fury*). A' this, a' this here! This house, claes, food in your belly . . . I'm buildin' this, an' you're my wife . . . My wife . . . What mair do you want . . . What mair is there?

CATHERINE (*quietly*). The city . . . The city that lies inside a man . . .

RAB (*witheringly*). What's this? (WILLIE COLE *has entered the yard. He stands idly, whistling, reading a newspaper.*) I've nae time . . .

CATHERINE. Don't go . . . No' like this . . .

RAB. Aye, like this! See where talkin' gets you . . . (*More gently.*) I'll no' be long . . . Into the town an' back . . . I'll no' be long . . . (*Goes out into yard.*)

CATHERINE (*alone*). There's nothin' here . . . Nothin' . . .

In the yard RAB *sees* WILLIE COLE *standing idly.*

RAB. What the hell are you playin' at?

WILLIE. I'm no' doin' nothin', Rab.

RAB. An' why the hell no'? You should be up the road gettin' loadit . . . You'll lose me work!

WILLIE. It's no' my fault, Rab son, honest t'God . . . Matt tellt me . . .

RAB. Matt?

WILLIE. He tellt me tae wait on till he found another load . . . Said he was after a bigger rate for the work . . . I thocht he would hae tellt you . . .

RAB. Aye well, if Matt said to wait on . . .

WILLIE. He did, Rab, aye . . . What could I dae? My hands are tied.

RAB. Away you go an' mind the pumps . . . On you go! I'm no' payin' money for you to read the paper . . .

WILLIE. Richt you are, boss. (*Exits.*)

RAB *goes towards the office, stops, changes his mind, exits.*

CATHERINE, *alone in the kitchen, gathers up her wool.*

TOMMY *and* JEAN CAIRNEY *enter the yard.* TOMMY *is a slender, poorly dressed boy of sixteen, with the speech and manner of a young child. He carries a hastily gathered bunch of flowers.* JEAN, *his mother, is a striking woman of forty, stern with herself and others. Her features have been coarsened by a lifetime spent working in the fields. Her clothes are plain and work-soiled.*

They enter the kitchen, unseen by CATHERINE. TOMMY *goes silently to* CATHERINE, *tickles her neck with the flowers.*

CATHERINE (*delighted*). Tommy? (*Turns to see him.*) It is . . . Come here my handsome man . . . (*embraces him tenderly, making him laugh.*) It's good to see you . . . You an' a', Jean . . . Come away in.

JEAN (*brusquely*). We'll no' stay long . . . I've tae go an' see tae th'auld Duncan woman . . .

CATHERINE. It's kind of you to come.

JEAN. It was Tommy wanted tae drop by . . . He'll no' go by wi'out comin' in to see you . . .

CATHERINE. I hope you wanted to come an' a', Jean. (TOMMY *hands flowers to* CATHERINE.) You're the soul o' love, so you are.

JEAN. Never heed him, Mrs Reid.

CATHERINE. Catherine . . . You surely ken that.

JEAN. Aye well, they're maistly weeds.

TOMMY (*laughing*). Aye . . . M-maistly weeds . . .

CATHERINE (*to* TOMMY.) I've missed you . . . Where have you been hiding?

TOMMY. Maistly weeds.

JEAN. I've been workin' in Grier's fields . . . He's no happy less he has you drippin' blood . . .

CATHERINE. You'll hae been at his mother's.

JEAN. Oh aye – he'll gie me an hour tae see tae his mother . . . Tae licht her a fire an' wipe her backside . . . There's no' a man in the world'll dae that.

CATHERINE. An' noo' the Duncan woman an' a'?

JEAN. Aye, an' there's others tae.

CATHERINE. You make me ashamed.

JEAN. What for ashamed?

CATHERINE. I dinnae look near any o' them.

JEAN. There's ay someone'll dae they things.

CATHERINE. I'll mak' us tea . . .

JEAN (firmly). No, no' for me. Thank-you.

CATHERINE. Then I've somethin' for Tommy . . . I ken what he likes . . .

TOMMY. Apple . . .

CATHERINE (giving him apple). There you go.

TOMMY. Apple.

JEAN. Aye well, what do you say?

TOMMY. Thank-you.

CATHERINE. Have you been workin', Tommy?

TOMMY. Thank-you, Catherine . . .

CATHERINE. Have you been workin' alang wi' your mother?

TOMMY. Apple . . .

JEAN. Wha in God's name would gie work tae a daunert wee bauchle the likes o' him?

CATHERINE. You're that bloody hard, Jean . . . (To TOMMY.) It's no' right . . .

TOMMY (laughing). Bauchle . . .

JEAN. Aye, it's richt enough . . . He sits at the side o' the field an' watches, or he taks a wander . . . He's a better life than the maist o' us.

CATHERINE. The things you say . . . (*To* TOMMY.) She's some woman, is she no'?

TOMMY (*laughing, spluttering apple*). Auld b-bitch . . .

JEAN. Look at the state o' you . . . Come on here till I wipe your face . . . (*Wipes his face.*) Only boy I ken can wash his face wi' an apple . . . You're no' a bairn ony mair . . . You're a man gettin' . . . Away an' see if you can eat like yin.

TOMMY. M-man. (*Takes a measured bite.*)

CATHERINE. You're a guid boy.

TOMMY (*serious*). Man.

JEAN. You've Matt hame.

CATHERINE. Aye.

JEAN. He's no' well, I hear.

CATHERINE (*shrugs*). He's a different man one minute tae the next . . . He's workin' . . .

JEAN. Workin'?

CATHERINE. He's in wi' Rab noo' . . .

JEAN. He was ay some boy for gettin' things the way he wanted . . . On you come, Tommy . . .

CATHERINE. Dinnae go yet, Jean . . . Matt's no' far . . . I'll shout on him . . .

JEAN (*firmly*). No, we're no' needin' that . . . There's nae guid in takin' a body awa frae their work . . .

CATHERINE. Stay, Jean . . . Talk . . .

JEAN. Whaur's the guid in that?

CATHERINE. I'll go mad . . . You're a' the same . . .

JEAN. Same as wha?

CATHERINE. Dinnae make me ask for your kindness . . . I count you as a friend, Jean . . . You an' Tommy baith . . . You come an' see me . . . We've laughed th'gither . . .

JEAN. I'm no' sayin' ony different.

CATHERINE. Then how is it every time it's like you dinnae ken me, an' we've tae start again right frae the beginnin'?

JEAN. I've no' ay the time for talk . . .

CATHERINE. Talkin' cannae hurt.

JEAN. Aye, it can hurt.

CATHERINE. You're a' that mad keen tae be hard . . .

JEAN. Life maks you hard.

CATHERINE (*lost for words*). Ach, Jean . . .

TOMMY. Talk . . . talk . . .

JEAN (*to* CATHERINE.) What do you want tae talk aboot?

CATHERINE. Aw, bugger it, I'm no' sure noo' . . . You stand there as hard as stane, so you dae . . . By the time I put a crack in you, I'm a' jingled.

JEAN (*laughing, yielding*). Aye, I can see that.

CATHERINE. There're times when I'm for runnin' back to the city . . . I sit quiet an' plan it, I dae . . . But I've nae home there . . . She's moved on . . . My mother . . . Some man, another man . . . I've nae address for my mother . . .

JEAN. It's time you made your ain hame in this house.

CATHERINE. How, Jean? How's that done?

JEAN. I'm no' the woman tae ask about that.

CATHERINE. How do you put up wi' it? The way you live . . . The things folk say . . .

JEAN. What? The wild woman that's up a' nicht dancin' wi' tinkers? The dirty witch wha lives alane wi' her punishment sent doon frae above? (*Touches* TOMMY'*s arm gently*.) Aye, words can hurt, but I've heard them a' noo'.

CATHERINE. I didnae mean to make you mind they things . . .

JEAN. Costs me nothin'.

CATHERINE. In the day, Jean, mair an' mair, I go for a sleep . . . I curl up under the top blanket, make mysel' that small you wouldnae could tell I was there . . . I just close down, an' when I wake it's like I'm half-drowned . . .

JEAN. It's fine for some . . .

CATHERINE. Aye . . . I didnae think it would be like this . . .

JEAN. Nothin's ever much the way you think . . . (*Bluntly, without self-pity.*) When I was a lassie there was a woman would go round seein' tae the auld yins . . . We'd run at her back shoutin' an' throwin' muck . . . An' noo' that woman's me . . . It's how it's come tae be, an' that's a' there is about it . . . (*Laughs.*) An' they're no' daft, the auld yins . . . They ken fine that as like as no' I'll be the woman tae haud the mirror tae their mouths . . .

CATHERINE. Jean, you are, you're hard.

JEAN. Awa' an' sleep.

TAM *enters the yard, sprawls on the ground by an old engine, raids it for parts.*

CATHERINE. I've done nothin' but I'm that tired . . .

JEAN. Nae wunner, wi' twa men in the house . . . The only thing better than twa men is yin, an' you're better yet wi' nane . . . (WILLIE COLE *enters the yard. He stands idly, smoking and reading his newspaper.*) On you go an' sleep if it's what you're needin' . . .

CATHERINE. I think I will . . .

TOMMY. Aye, sleep . . .

CATHERINE. You're a soul . . .

TOMMY. Night-night, Catherine.

CATHERINE (*laughing, sleepy*). Aye, night-night, Tommy . . . (*Kisses him.*) Dinnae be so long next time . . . Dinnae be so long . . . (*Goes into the house.*)

JEAN. Come here you . . . (TOMMY *obeys, and she sorts his clothes.*) It's a losin' battle . . . (*With irony.*) Soul!

They go out into the yard.

WILLIE (*in mock terror*). Jean Cairney! Christ, I must be deid or deein' . . . Help me, Tam . . .

TOMMY. Tammy Burnet, Tammy Burnet . . .

TAM. Aye, I see you fine.

TOMMY *gets down beside him, watches him work.*

WILLIE (*to* JEAN.) Whaur's a' your fancy-men the day then?

JEAN. They'll a' be in bed wi' your sister.

WILLIE (*stung, bested*). That's rubbish that . . . Nae need for it . . . (*Spits, looks away.*)

JEAN. You're a clown, Willie Cole . . . (*To* TOMMY.) Come on, son.

TOMMY. Stay . . . Want to stay . . .

WILLIE. He cannae stay here . . . No' him . . .

TAM. How no'?

WILLIE. He'll be in the way.

TAM. The way o' what?

WILLIE. My work.

TAM (*to* TOMMY.) We're talkin' miracles noo'. (*To* JEAN.) Aye, he can stay.

JEAN. Thank-you . . . I'll be back for him. (*Goes.*)

WILLIE. She'd put the fear o' God in you, that woman . . . It's a muzzle she's needin' . . .

TAM. Aye, but she's some worker . . . An' Grier's no' saft on her . . . She's as guid as ony man . . . (WILLIE *has gone back to his newspaper.*) A damnt sicht better than some . . .

WILLIE. Awa' . . . I've still t'be tellt my duties.

TAM. A guid worker doesnae need t'be tellt.

WILLIE. Aye he does . . . It a' requires tae come frae the tap doon . . . But we've the richt gaffer noo', have we no' just? Can you no' feel the change? We've the richt gaffer noo'.

TAM. We'll see.

TOMMY *leans over a tyre, rocks himself back and forth.*

WILLIE. Mind you, it's no' ay ways the way o' it . . . (*Indicates newspaper.*) There's guid men on their bendit knee for work an' a' these gaffers'll gie them is blethers . . . Wavin' like royalty, gettin' in an' out o' big motors . . . You'd think when a gang o' educated men get th'gither an' cry themselves the government events would be made to happen for the better instead o' the worse . . . You'd think guid events would come to pass . . . But nae body pays ony heed tae the opinion o' the likes o' me . . . Mair's the pity, mair's the pity . . . (*Turns page, reads.*) Parachutes.

TAM. What?

WILLIE. Parachutes . . . 'The New Soldier' it says here – 'Death from the air' . . . They just drap you out a plane . . . Death frae the air, richt enough . . . (*Folds paper, puts it in his pocket.*) So is this it, then? Is this my life? (*No reply. TOMMY begins to hum and sing dreamily as he rocks backwards and forwards.*) Could you be quiet, son? You're gettin' on my nerves . . . (TOMMY *is quiet.*) This is where I live an' this is where I'll die . . . We'll be in this wilderness a' our days, countin' the pennies alang wi' the days . . .

TAM. Awa' tae the city an' tak' your greetin' face wi' you . . .

WILLIE. An' whaur's the purpose in that when there's guid men beggin' in the street while their bairns cry out wi' hunger? It's a cryin' bloody shame, an' it's the government's tae blame! So it is, it's the government's tae blame . . .

TOMMY. Wha's the government?

WILLIE. That's no' richt put, son . . .

MATT *comes out of the office, fierce with energy, his greatcoat flying open around him. He grips some papers like a weapon.*

MATT. Willie, get in your wagon an' awa' up the road t'Inchinnan! Here's your lines . . . (*Hands papers to him.*) Move yoursel'!

TOMMY (*cowering*). G-government . . .

TAM. Naw, naw, son . . .

MATT. Foot doon noo'! Back here loadit the nicht . . . It's tae leave first thing!

WILLIE (*reading load-lines*). For London?

MATT. Aye for London! There'll be nae mair jukin' about, nae mair bits an' pieces . . .

WILLIE (*to TAM.*) Did I no' tell you? We've the richt gaffer noo' . . .

MATT. You an' a', Tam . . . Awa' up wi' him an' help wi' the loadin' . . .

TAM. I'll need tae ask Rab . . .

MATT. I'll speak tae him! Move yoursels! We're in wi' the big boys noo' . . . On your way!

WILLIE. Did I no' tell you . . . Did I no' tell you? (*Goes hurriedly with* TAM.)

MATT (*shouts after them*). Foot tae the floor and back loadit the nicht! I gie'd the man my word an' by Christ he'll see I'm as guid as my word! You're workin' for a Reid, mind that . . . (*He sits on an oil drum, exhausted by his triumph.*) A man learns tae tak' what he wants . . . (*Takes out a half bottle, drinks.*) If it's no' there he looks till he finds it . . .

TOMMY (*warily*). G-government . . .

MATT (*startled, seeing him for the first time*). Guid God, whaur the hell did you jump frae? (TOMMY *backs away.*) You've nae need tae be frichtened . . . Come here . . . Come on noo' . . . (TOMMY *comes closer.*) What's your name? (*No answer.*) Tell me your name . . .

TOMMY. Tommy . . .

MATT. Wha dae you belong tae?

TOMMY. T-Tommy . . .

MATT. Tommy wha? Wha's your faither?

TOMMY. T-Tamson . . .

MATT. What Tamson's that?

TOMMY. Jock Tamson.

MATT. You wouldnae be tryin' tae mak a monkey out o' me, would you?

TOMMY (*laughing, pulling at* MATT'*s hand*). M-monkey . . .

MATT. So you are a wee monkey . . .

TOMMY (*pushing hard against* MATT'*s hand*). Strong . . . Strong . . .

MATT. Aye, you're a strong laddie, there's nae doubt o' that . . .

TOMMY (*pushing harder*). Strong . . .

MATT. That's enough noo', son.

TOMMY. Strong!

MATT. Enough, I'm sayin'!

TOMMY *lets go, moves away.*

TOMMY. See me . . . Tricks . . . Can dae tricks . . . (*Rolls head over heels.*)

MATT. Very guid, very guid . . . Mair . . . (*Drinks as* TOMMY *performs another trick.*) Again . . . (TOMMY *repeats his last trick, grins with pride.*) We'll need tae pit you in the circus . . .

TOMMY. See me . . . See me . . .

MATT. I see you fine . . .

TOMMY (*taking hold of* MATT *again*). Guid at tricks . . .

MATT. Aye, an' let that be the finish o' it.

TOMMY. Strong . . . Strong . . .

MATT (*invaded, angry*). I said – finish! (*Pushes* TOMMY *away, drinks.*) I didnae mean tae mak you sair . . . You're in some state . . . Could you no' tidy yoursel' up?

Enter JEAN *unseen by* MATT *and* TOMMY.

TOMMY. My mother doesnae love me . . .

MATT. Wha in God's name put that notion in your heid?

TOMMY (*laughing*). She t-tellt me . . .

JEAN. Here, you! Come here when you're tellt! (TOMMY *runs to her.*)

MATT. Jean . . .

JEAN. I hope he's no' kept you back.

MATT. Is it Jean Cairney?

JEAN. It is.

MATT (*enjoying the sound of the name*). Jean Cairney.

JEAN. Matthew Reid . . . Welcome hame.

MATT. Christ, I would hardly hae kent you . . .

JEAN. I've had mony a year wi' the wind in my face.

MATT. Aye, there's that . . .

TOMMY. Did my tricks, did my tricks . . .

MATT. He's your boy.

JEAN. He's mine.

MATT. He's a fine boy.

TOMMY. M-man . . . Strong . . .

MATT. He says you're no' awfy fond o' him.

TOMMY. So she's no'.

JEAN. He's in love wi' the hale world . . . He'll need tae learn it'll no' love him back.

MATT. Aye, there's that an' a' . . . (*To* TOMMY.) You listen to your mother . . . (*Drinks.*)

JEAN. What are you doin' back here, in this house?

MATT. The takin' on o' the world, it's no' been easy . . . I've come hame, Jean . . .

JEAN. Whaur's hame for you noo'?

MATT. I thocht that way mysel', but it's worked fine for me a' the same, this comin' hame . . .

JEAN. It's a place like ony other.

MATT. No, Jean . . . Just seein' you standin' there an' I can breathe mair easy . . . I've a hunger I've no' felt for years . . . A hunger for a' that's tae come . . .

JEAN. An' what's tae come for you, Matt?

MATT. I've a place here . . . Alang wi' Rab . . . I can see a way tae help him on . . .

JEAN. What hae you got tae gie your brother?

MATT. He's done well, he's come up, but I can tak' it the hale way . . . (*Taps his head.*) In here, he's still a worker . . .

JEAN. An' he's tae be blamed for that?

MATT. You've tae be hard wi' a business, that's just the way o' it . . . This is hame right enough . . . It's been waitin' for me a' my life . . . (*Drinks.*)

JEAN. So there stands Matt Reid, the big man, the great
   drinker, the bonny fechter wha once sorted the Monkton
   boys . . . Aye, an' I see you yet in your uniform, hame on
   leave, a'body buyin' you drink, cryin' you hero . . .

TOMMY (*excited*). Sojer, sojer . . .

JEAN. How you loved the uniform . . . You learned tae smile
   like it was a favour . . .

MATT. An' whaur's the Jean Cairney I mind? You were ay that
   quiet an' gentle . . .

JEAN. Is that a' you mind o' me?

MATT. I mind you best as a young lassie in the school, your
   face ay at the back, heid down in case yon tyrant Duncan
   came roun' tae you . . . Mind how for a punishment he'd
   mak ye stand an' sing . . . You never liked tae speak up . . .

JEAN. No' like some . . .

MATT. I could ay speak up for mysel' . . . But you . . . A' I had
   tae dae was luk roun' an' there you'd be, lukkin' on just . . .

JEAN. You took some watchin' . . .

MATT. It felt guid . . . Like my mother wasnae deid, or I had a
   sister, or maybe yin day . . . It's daft, I ken, wi' you there in
   front o' me, but I'm shair I could luk ower my shoulder an'
   see you yet . . . (*Shivers.*)

JEAN. Just you keep lukkin' roun' if that's a' you mind o'
   me . . . (*To* TOMMY.) It's time we were hame . . .

MATT. Have you a man at your hame, Jean?

JEAN. I've nae need o' a man . . . (*Goes to leave.*)

MATT. Wait, Jean . . .

JEAN. Keep haud o' a' that strength o' yours for it's plain tae
   me you've no' muckle left . . .

MATT. Awa' woman! What's that you're sayin' . . .

JEAN. There stands Matt Reid . . . (*More gently.*) There's yin
   door we a' come tae at nicht . . .

MATT. What kin' o' words are they? (JEAN *leaves, he shouts
   after her.*) Come back here till I tell you . . . I'm as strong
   as ever I was!

TOMMY. Strong . . .

MATT (*continuing to shout after* JEAN). What kin' o' welcome's this for a man . . . It's hellish what the years'll dae tae a woman! (TOMMY *exits, after his mother.*) You're a madwoman! I'm as strong as ever I was . . . (*He pulls his greatcoat off, flings it away, and goes to a tap. He catches water in his hands, splashes it vigorously against his face. Tremors shake his body. He places his head under the tap, stands and shakes his head like a dog. As he smooths the wet hair from his face the lights fade slowly in the yard outside until it is night. Enter* CATHERINE. *She hands him a towel.*) Thanking you, Mistress Reid . . . How is he?

CATHERINE. He's angry . . .

MATT. You should stay wi' him if he's angry . . . Tae Hell, it'll pass . . .

CATHERINE. You're that sure o' yoursel' . . .

MATT. Aye, I'm shair . . .

CATHERINE. You should hae talked wi' him first . . . He'd hae wanted that . . .

MATT. He'd hae wanted it, aye.

CATHERINE. You owe him that . . .

MATT. I owe naebody nothin' . . . No' in this life . . .

CATHERINE. He used to be that gentle . . .

MATT. You've tae be strong t'be gentle . . . You need tae see the change frae yin tae the other . . . The layin' down o' the hammer . . . There's worth in it then . . .

CATHERINE. He's ay been kind . . .

MATT. There's nothin' gentle about the weak.

Enter RAB.

RAB. You're there, Matt . . . (*Turns away, too angry to speak.*)

MATT. Come awa' in, Rab . . . Come awa' through . . .

RAB. I've nae argument about the London load . . . You've got a better rate than I would hae thocht possible, but there was nae need tae speak tae Shaw Wilson the way you did . . .

MATT (*with contempt*). Shaw Wilson.

RAB. He gied me my first load.

MATT. You've had your last load frae him.

RAB. There was nae need tae cry him down the way you did! He gied me regular work, kept me goin' . . .

MATT. A' the bits an' pieces naebody else would touch . . . I phoned roun', I checked up . . . The bugger was laughin' up his sleeve, the rate he was payin' you . . . You'd hae been cheaper no' workin' . . .

RAB. It doesnae matter a damn! It was an arrangement I had! It was my business!

MATT. Where's the guid in a' this, Rab son? A business is there tae be worked, no' worked for . . . You're like a man in his grave . . .

RAB. I like tae go at my ain speed!

MATT. I'm on your side, Rab . . . I owe you . . . We can build it th'gither . . . If we dae richt by this London end, they'll gie us mair work, regular work, an' we'll buy twa maybe three new wagons a year . . . (CATHERINE *gently strokes* RAB*'s head.*) In no time we'll hae a fleet o' wagons . . . Is that no' a grand word . . . What do you say, noo'? What do you say to that?

CATHERINE (*gently*). Come on by, Rab . . .

RAB. You can lose yoursel' . . .

MATT. You've tae be hard . . . Push on . . . Yin nicht I slept in a shed by a railway . . . In the morn the twa boys I was wi' were deid, deid wi' the cold . . . I took the coat frae yin an' the boots frae the other an' went on my road tae yin place an' another, till I was here, till I was standin' here . . .

CATHERINE. Come on by . . .

MATT. In France, Rab, you should hae seen the officers . . . No much older than me, some o' them, shavers just, but they could fairly tell you what t'dae . . . Nae need tae shout, a word here, a smile there, an' you'd dae onythin' they wanted . . . Aye, an' it would hae felt like an honour . . .

To expect tae get what you want . . . That's where we've tae
learn . . .

RAB. Can we, Matt? Can we build it th'gither?

CATHERINE (*continuing to stroke* RAB*'s head*). You're
tired . . . Come on by wi' me . . .

MATT. Aye, we can build it . . . The wagon's loadit an' ready . . .
I tellt their boss you'd be bringin' it down yoursel' . . .
Mister Robert Reid . . . (*He goes behind* CATHERINE,
*caresses her neck. She is confused, tormented, but she does
not resist.*) They'll want tae see the kin' o' man they're
dealin' wi' . . . They'll want tae get your measure . . . He'll
no' be disappointed . . . You'll be a new man at the finish
up . . . An officer . . . (*He moves away from* CATHERINE.)
The wagon's loadit an' ready . . .

RAB. Havin' you in wi' me, Rab, I'm no' sure if I'm twice or
half the man . . .

MATT. We'll build it th'gither.

RAB. I've somethin' tae show you, Matt . . . I've had it
ordered . . . (*Makes to go.*)

CATHERINE. Don't go . . .

RAB. I've it through here . . . I want you tae see it . . . (*Exits,
into the house.*)

MATT *goes over to* CATHERINE, *takes hold of her, kisses
her. They break apart just as* RAB *enters carrying a parcel.*

RAB (*tearing off the wrapping paper*). I'm keen tae see what
you mak' o' it . . . The boy's made a richt guid job . . . He's
done it the way I tellt him . . . Bricht an' clear . . . (*He
reveals a brightly painted metal sign that bears the words –*
REID BROTHERS.) What dae you think tae that? I'll hae it
put richt at the front o' the wagons . . . I'll hae it at the gate
tae the yard . . .

MATT. That's guid o' you, Rab son . . . Kind . . . (*He takes the
sign from* RAB.) I owe you . . . But I'll need tae see . . .
I wouldnae want a partner at my back wha wasnae ready
tae go the hale way . . . You could be awa' the nicht . . .
You'd mak guid time . . . You'll hae the open road in front
o' you . . .

RAB. I could be broken, Matt . . .

MATT. On you go, Rab son . . . It's loadit an' waitin' . . .

RAB (*to himself*). A' my life . . .

MATT. Some men are broken afore they're born!

RAB *takes his jacket and goes to the door.*

CATHERINE. Rab . . .

RAB. Is it possible some men enjoy their dreams . . . When they're lyin' back, near tae sleep . . . Is it possible? . . . (*He leaves the house, crosses the yard, and exits.*)

MATT *sits exhausted in a chair. He holds a hand out to* CATHERINE. *She looks at him.*

Fade lights.

Act Three

The yard and the kitchen. Late afternoon. TAM *enters the yard, cleans and packs away his tools.*

CATHERINE *sleeps, curled up in a chair in the kitchen. She wears a pretty dress, but has no shoes on her feet and her hair is unbrushed.*

WILLIE *enters the yard, hums, dances a few steps.*

WILLIE. Can you see me,Tam? Can you no' just see me?

TAM. I'm no' blin' . . . I see you fine . . .

WILLIE. No' here, no' the noo . . . The nicht, in Grier's barn, at the dancin' . . .

TAM. You'll be up, will you?

WILLIE. I'll be up among them on the flair, so I will . . . Mind you, you've tae be gey bloody vigilant . . .

TAM. How vigilant?

WILLIE. The womenfolk . . . You can ask a lassie up an' the next thing you ken you're standin' in the kirk wi' a ticht collar on . . .

TAM. You're safe enough, Willie.

WILLIE. There's nane o' us safe frae that . . . No' wi' drink taken . . .

TAM. There'll be nae drink the nicht . . .

CATHERINE *stirs and wakes. She sees her shoes on the floor, and picks them up, then sits wearily with the shoes forgotten in her lap.*

WILLIE. How no'?

TAM. You need wages for drink.

WILLIE. We've never no' been paid . . . Matt'll pay us . . .

TAM (*impatiently*). How can he pay us when he's no' here?

WILLIE. He'll be back . . . (*Sees that* TAM *doesn't believe him.*) Aye, he will . . . He'll hae a lot on his mind . . . Runnin' a business . . .

TAM. Nae doubt . . .

WILLIE. In the office . . . Rab ay has the wages ready for liftin'.

TAM. You cannae just tak them . . .

WILLIE. How no'? They're ours tae tak . . . (*Goes towards office.*)

TAM. You'll need a key . . .

WILLIE. I ken wha'll hae a key . . .

TAM. Leave her in peace, Willie.

WILLIE. How?

TAM. Just.

WILLIE. Tae hell wi' that . . . (*Knocks on door, and* CATHERINE *stands hopefully.*) Mistress Reid . . . (*Enters.*)

CATHERINE (*disappointed*). Willie Cole . . .

WILLIE (*with a mischievous bow*). The man o' your dreams . . .

CATHERINE. Go away . . . Please . . .

WILLIE (*firmly*). As soon as I'm paid, I'll go . . .

CATHERINE. Matt'll pay you . . .

WILLIE. Matt's gone.

CATHERINE (*urgently*). Gone where? Tell me . . . (TAM *enters the house*.)

WILLIE. Aye well, that's a mystery, Mistress Reid . . .

TAM. He went out the yard like he was in a dream . . . I shouted after him, but it made nae difference . . . It was like he'd heard some other voice . . .

WILLIE. But there was nae other voice . . .

TAM. No' that we could hear onyway . . .

WILLIE. A mystery richt enough . . .

CATHERINE. You'll get your money in the office . . . (*Takes a key from a hook, offers it to* WILLIE.)

WILLIE (*Not accepting the key*). I ken it's a nuisance, but it micht be best if you gied them out . . . It's ay best tae keep things richt . . . (CATHERINE *puts on her shoes*.) My, you're a picture . . .

TAM. Willie!

WILLIE. It would brak your heart just tae luk at her . . . Easy done . . . You'll be at the dance the nicht . . . (*She looks away from him.*) Do you no' ken about it? The hale village'll be there . . . Grier lets us hae his barn, same time every year . . . There'll be a band playin' . . . Fancy no' kennin' that . . .

TAM. Rab'll no' hae forgot . . . It's a lang road but he's had twa days for it . . .

WILLIE (*with an edge*). Aye, twa days an' twa nichts . . . Fully . . .

TAM (*kindly*). He'll be back, an' if he's no', we'll be there . . . There'll ay be a kent face . . .

CATHERINE (*treasuring his kindness*). Thank-you, Tam . . .

WILLIE. Or Matt could tak you . . . (CATHERINE *walks past him, out to the yard, followed by* WILLIE *and* TAM.) You'd mak a fine pair . . . They'd mak room for you on the flair, so they would . . . They'd a' stand back an' gie you your place . . . (*The door, unlocked, opens for* CATHERINE *without a key. She enters. The sound of glass breaking underfoot.)*

TAM. Guid God . . .

WILLIE (*at the doorway, kicking at broken glass*). His desk an' chair in bits . . . A' thing scattered tae the winds . . . Wha's done this? (CATHERINE *emerges from the office. She seems elated.*) Papers a'where . . . A' Rab's documents . . . (*Picks up small tin box.*) The money-box . . . Empty . . .

CATHERINE (*taking hold absent-mindedly of* TAM*'s arm*). Some men have nae need o' offices . . .

TAM (*concerned for her*). Mrs Reid?

CATHERINE. I'm very well . . . Really, I am . . . Thank-you . . .

WILLIE. His auld lamp's smashed an' a' . . . At nicht you could see Rab at the windae . . . Seein' tae his documents . . .

TAM. Quiet, Willie . . .

CATHERINE. He'll come back . . . I know he will . . .

WILLIE. Wha's done this?

Enter TOMMY, *at a run, breathless and over-excited. He runs to* CATHERINE.

TOMMY (*speaking almost too fast to be understood*). The best . . . The best thing, C-Catherine . . . Met him on the road . . . Walkin', walkin' . . . Met him on the road . . .

CATHERINE. Ssh, now, Tommy . . . Quiet . . .

TOMMY (*racing on*). Up an' up an' up an' up . . .

TAM. Slow doon, son . . .

TOMMY (*Running to* TAM). Met him on the road, Tammy Burnet . . . Tammy Burnet, I did . . . Took me up the hill . . . Up an' up . . .

WILLIE. Wha did?

TOMMY (*points off*). Him . . . Him . . . (*Laughing.*) G-government . . .

Enter MATT, *excited, a little breathless, as if he has shared* TOMMY*'S pleasure.* TOMMY *runs to him.*

CATHERINE. Matt . . .

MATT (*turning away from her*). Never heed me . . .

TOMMY. Up an' up an' up . . .

MATT. Tae the very tap o' Pollock's Hill . . .

TOMMY. L-laid me doon an' gied me a push . . . I rolled on doon the hill . . . Faster'n' faster'n faster till the up was doon an' the doon was up . . .

MATT. He wasnae feart . . . No' him . . .

TOMMY. Faster'n faster . . .

MATT. He reaches the flat an' he's up runnin' for mair . . .

TOMMY. Mair, mair!

MATT. Up he runs like a wild animal . . . Again, he says . . . Again . . .

TOMMY (*laughing, spinning on his heel*). The blue turnt tae green an' the green tae blue till it was a' yin . . . A' yin . . . (*Stops spinning, stands dizzily.*) P-picked me up frae the grun' . . . Strong . . . Strong . . .

MATT. A wild animal . . . (*Catches the look of* TAM *and* WILLIE.) An' what hae you found tae stare at? The day's near done . . . Awa' hame wi' you!

TAM. We've been in the office, Matt . . .

MATT. An' what richt hae you tae go in there? What business is that o' yours?

TAM. We're needin' paid, or are you no' up tae that?

MATT. I'll gie you paid . . . Pair o' bloody clowns . . . (*Searches through the pockets of his greatcoat.*) I'll gie you paid if it's paid you're after . . . You're workin' for a Reid, mind that . . . You're workin' for a Reid . . . (*Finds two crumpled wage packets, throws them to the ground.*) There! Tak them, for a' the guid they'll dae you . . .

They're too proud and angry to pick them up. TAM *finally steps forward to retrieve them.*

CATHERINE. No, Tam . . . (*She picks them up, gives them to* WILLIE *and* TAM.)

WILLIE. My yin's been opened . . .

MATT. Count it! Go on! Christ, Willie Cole . . . When you fa'
intae the dark it'll no mak ony difference for you've lived in
the dark a' your life . . . You're a pair pathetic bloody cratur,
a weasel by Christ, an' I'll tell you how I ken . . . You
believed in me . . . In me . . . Ye bloody clown ye . . .
(*Drinks from a half bottle.*)

WILLIE (*more hurt than he can show*). I'll no' be countin' it . . .
(*Pockets his wages.*) There'll be nae need o' that, I'm
shair . . . But I will say this, Matt son . . . If your faither
could see you the day he'd be hertsair at the state o' you, for
he could ay keep a civil tongue in his heid . . .

MATT. Awa' hame . . . You've been paid . . .

WILLIE. I'll no listen tae this . . . Come on, Tam . . .

MATT. Awa' tae your dance . . .

TAM *and* WILLIE *go to leave, but* TAM *stops by*
CATHERINE.

WILLIE. Never heed her . . .

CATHERINE (*answering* TAM*'s unspoken question*). I'll be
fine . . . Thank-you . . .

MATT. An' why should she no' be? Answer me that!

TAM (to CATHERINE.) There'll ay be a kent face . . . (*She
nods gratefully.*) If you're shair . . .

CATHERINE. I am . . . Thank-you . . . (TAM *and* WILLIE
go.) You tried to leave, but you couldnae . . . You came
back . . .

MATT. Ssh . . . Can you hear it?

TOMMY. Tommy hears it . . .

MATT. You must hear it . . .

CATHERINE. There's nothin' . . .

MATT. The wind, the wind . . . The child o' heaven . . . The
king o'the fields . . .

CATHERINE. You came back to me . . . Take me to the dance,
Matt . . . We'll go th'gither . . .

TOMMY. Dance, dance . . .

MATT. I tell you stories . . . You like that . . .

CATHERINE. The city that lies inside a man . . .

MATT. Stories . . .

CATHERINE. Some men are strong enough to live the way they want . . .

TOMMY. S-stories . . .

Enter JEAN, *unseen by any of them.*

CATHERINE. Can you see a' their faces in Grier's barn when you come in wi' me on your arm?

MATT. Wi' you on my arm . . . I'd dance you aff your feet . . .

JEAN. An' would you dance wi' me, Matt? (TOMMY *runs to her.*)

MATT. Jean Cairney . . . Are you askin'?

JEAN. Would I need tae ask?

MATT. I'd dance wi' you . . .

JEAN (*wiping* TOMMY*'s face with her sleeve*). It's no' like him be this lang frae my side . . .

TOMMY. Up, up the hill . . . It was the best . . .

MATT. I had money . . . I had the road under my feet . . . An' then I met that wild boy o' yours . . . I was near clean awa' . . .

JEAN. Whaur tae? Yon place whaur nane o' us come back frae . . .

MATT. Get her the hell awa'! (*Hugs himself in pain.*)

JEAN. Are you weakenin', Matt?

CATHERINE. What is it, Jean?

JEAN (*still to* MATT). Aye . . . An' the nicht'll be closin' in aroun' you like a frien' . . .

CATHERINE. What do you want frae him? . . . What's he tae you? . . .

TOMMY *goes to* MATT, *touches his arm gently, consolingly.*

TOMMY. Sojer . . . Strong . . .

CATHERINE (*to* JEAN, *as if understanding*). Tommy?

JEAN. No, no . . . Tommy's no' his if that's what you're
thinkin' . . . (*Laughs.*) No' in the way you'd think onyway . . .

CATHERINE (*keenly*). How then?

JEAN. It's no' what you micht cry a big story . . .

CATHERINE. Tell me.

JEAN. Oh, it micht hae been that a daft young lassie wanted
tae turn the heid o' the boy she dreamed o' . . . Had ay
dreamed o' . . . A handsome sojer-boy hame on leave . . .
An' it micht hae been that his proud heid wouldnae turn so
she thocht tae teach him his lesson by goin' wi' another . . .
A boy wi' a gentle way about him . . . Another sojer . . .
Some other pair bloody sojer-boy . . . Never even kent his
name, daft wee lassie that I was . . .

MATT. No, Jean . . .

JEAN. Did you no' ken, Matt . . . Did you no' ken I had you in
my dreams?

MATT. Ken it? No . . .

CATHERINE. You'll no' take him from me . . . I'll no' let
you . . .

JEAN (*fiercely*). Dinnae speak about what you cannae
understand! (*Relents, more gently.*) It'll no' be me that taks
him frae you . . .

MATT. Get her the hell awa'! (*He goes into the house, fights
against the pain that floods him.*)

CATHERINE (*like a prayer, to the heavens*). Don't take him
from me now . . . Don't give him to me and then take him
away . . .

JEAN. Hush now, lassie . . . (*Embraces her.*) There's nae
argument atween us twa . . . You're a guid lassie . . . (*Kisses
her head.*) He'll hae mixed his blood wi' yours an' when
you wake he'll be on his road . . .

CATHERINE (*through tears*). You're nothin' tae him . . .

JEAN. Hush now . . . Awa' in tae him . . .

CATHERINE. Nothin' . . .

JEAN. Awa' in . . . (CATHERINE *goes into the house.*
JEAN *touches* TOMMY*'s face gently.*) An' you're a guid
boy tae . . .

TOMMY. M-man . . . Strong . . .

JEAN. I ken he hears us . . . A house'll no' haud him . . .
(*Sings Softly.*)

I wid hae gi'en him my lips tae kiss,
Had I been his, had I been his;
Barley breid an' elder wine,
Had I been his as he is mine.

Hear me, Matt . . . You'll no' need tae be alane . . .
(*Embraces* TOMMY.) He'll come . . . A house'll no' haud
him . . . (*As she goes with* TOMMY.)

My beloved shall hae this hert tae break,
Reid, reid wine an' the barley cake,
A hert tae break, an' a mou' tae kiss,
Tho' he be nae mine, as I am his,

CATHERINE *goes to* MATT *but he turns away from her.*

MATT. There's nae heat in this house . . . What's wrang there's
nae heat? . . .

CATHERINE. I'll no' let you go . . .

MATT. He'd hae been better wi' the auld stanes . . . He should
o' built wi' the auld stanes . . . (*Shivers.*) There's nae peace
in houses . . . (*He offers her his bottle, which she refuses.
He pours a drink.*) A pity . . . A woman should smell o'
drink . . . (*She turns away in hurt and anger.*)

CATHERINE. I get twisted, Matt . . . Twisted up . . . (*She
touches his shoulder. He brings his glass down hard on the
table causing her to start with fright.*) The way you wanted
me . . . (*He brings his glass down hard on the table.*) Why
do you hurt me?

MATT. It feels guid the way you jump . . .

CATHERINE. You can be happy if you love each other a little
bit . . . (*He brings his glass down hard on the table.*)
And all you need is a little happiness and it starts all over
again . . .

MATT *takes a violent hold of her, forces the bottle to her mouth. She twists her mouth away, the whisky falling over her face.*

MATT. A woman should smell o' drink . . .

CATHERINE *strikes him. He looks at her, untouched.*
CATHERINE *matches his gaze, more than matches it, until*
MATT *looks away.*

CATHERINE. Mind me, Matt . . . Mind me . . .

MATT (*embraces her*). Your saft skin . . . Your saft claes on the flair like water . . .

CATHERINE. There's nothin' to be afraid o' . . . Feel how strong we are . . . We've broken the rules th'gither . . .

MATT. For some men there are nae rules . . .

CATHERINE. Yes!

MATT. For they've nothin' left tae live by . . . (*Pulls away from her.*)

CATHERINE. You can live how you like . . . When you're in love . . .

MATT. I'll leave this house . . .

CATHERINE. No . . .

MATT. I had money . . . I felt the road under me . . . Carryin' me on . . . It would be a mercy tae you, me leavin' this house . . . I'm a tramp . . . A thief . . . But wi' you . . . You shouldnae hae me under this roof . . .

CATHERINE. Weakness . . .

MATT (*sings quietly*). 'Oh, love, love, love' . . . A' this . . . I thocht I was entitled . . . But it's time I was on my way . . . I wish you a' happiness an' the luck tae fin' it . . . (*She holds onto him.*) Leave me . . . Leave me go in peace . . .

He pulls free of her, goes to leave, but she flings herself at him and clings on with fierce strength. He whirls round, roars with anguish, but she won't be dislodged.

The sound of an engine, which dies and ceases. MATT gives up his struggle, lets his arms hang lifelessly.
CATHERINE *finally lets go of him, turns away.*

CATHERINE. I'm stronger . . . Stronger than you a' . . .

MATT. Thank-you . . . For your kindness . . .

> RAB *crosses the yard and enters the house. He is alive with the feverish energy that sometimes comes with exhaustion.*

RAB (*after a pause*). It's a funny thing, Matt son, but I thocht you micht hae moved on by noo' . . . I've no' slept . . . I cannae mind what sleep is . . . I've nae need o' sleep . . . I'll no' be stayin' . . . I'm back up an' loadit . . . For the road again the nicht . . . The south . . . It's guid work, the London end . . . I've a lot tae thank you for . . . Their yard, it must hae been a mile across . . . The boss, he sent for me tae come up tae his office . . . Up the marble stairs tae his office . . . I could tell by the luk o' him he'd be happier wi' the soun' o' his ain voice . . . You never came up, Matt son . . . Reid Brothers . . . I never made mention o' my brother . . . Doon in the yard, outside his windae, the wagons went by, yin after the other . . . They never stopped . . . Frae a' ower they'd come . . . Just tae go by his windae . . . He comes up wi' a name for my business . . . Southern Transport . . . A suggestion, he says . . . I tellt him I had nothin' against it . . . Southern Transport . . . He'd taken a likin' tae me . . . I could see that . . . He sets me up wi' a return load, gies me a list o' names . . . Contacts he cried them . . . Offers me a' the work I can tak . . . Says how he's lukkin' forrit t'doin' business wi' me . . . It's a pleasure, I tellt him . . . A pleasure . . . Southern Transport . . . It's a funny thing, Matt son, but I thocht you micht hae moved on . . . I thocht you micht hae been on your way . . .

MATT. There stands Robert Reid talkin' tae his wife an' brother . . . His lovely young wife . . . Elder brother . . . Eldest son . . . Matthew Reid . . . Finest worker in the field . . . Horseman . . . A word for a'body . . . Well liked . . . Sojer-boy . . . Scared o' nothin' . . . Came back a man . . . (*Touches the clock.*) Marrit the lassie he loved . . . Done well for himsel' . . . Ain hame an' business . . . Ay kent he had it in him . . . Somethin' special . . . Marked him doon as that bit different . . . A respected man . . . Upstandin' . . . Fine young boys . . . A lassie tae . . . The very image . . . Loved an' respected . . . Matthew Reid . . .

RAB. I cannae mind it nae mair . . . Between you an' the horse, you a man an' me a boy . . . I cannae mind it nae mair . . . Are you still here, Matt son? . . . In my hame . . . I think maybe after a' you're just passin' through . . .

MATT. You've it a', Rab . . . (*Goes to leave.*)

RAB. Matt . . .

CATHERINE. We're nothin' tae him . . . Nothin' . . .

MATT. A' in the world that a man could want . . . (*Goes.*)

CATHERINE. Nothin' . . . I'll leave this house . . . I'll no' stay under its roof . . . (*Goes to leave.*)

RAB. Catherine! (*She stops.*) I've come . . . I've . . . Cannae fin' the words, Christ . . . I've come back for you . . . Nothin' else . . . Come awa' wi' me, Catherine . . . Doon the road in the wagon.

CATHERINE. Naeb'dy else'll hae me noo', is that it?

RAB. I want you tae come wi' me . . .

CATHERINE. Is that how you think tae keep a hold o' me?

The light in the clock begins to glow more brightly.

RAB. A' the time I was on the road I thocht o' you . . . Couldnae keep you out . . . I could talk to you then . . . Aye, I said it a' then . . .

CATHERINE. I'll leave this house . . .

RAB. A' I'm after is your happiness . . .

CATHERINE. I was happier breakin' what you'd built than I ever was watchin' you build it . . .

RAB. I'm askin' you tae come wi' me . . .

CATHERINE. Might be I'll no' come back . . .

RAB. Aye you'll come back . . . I made you a promise . . . I'll wait . . . Outside, I'll wait for you . . . Catherine . . . I'd be lost wi'out you . . . I can say nae mair than that . . . (*Goes, stands lost in the yard.*)

CATHERINE. You were the kindest, maist gentle man I'd ever met . . . But it might be I'll no' come back . . . (RAB *leaves the yard.*) It might happen that you'll stop an' leave me alone wi' mysel' . . . It might happen that I'll open my door, get out, an' walk away . . .

Fade lights.

Act Four

Night on a vast empty stage – Pollock's Hill. The light from the clock rises like a bright moon in the midst of darkness.

Enter TOMMY, *excited.*

TOMMY. Up an' up an' up . . . (*Enter* JEAN *and* MATT, *who is weary, unsteady.*) Tae the tap . . . Richt tae the tap . . .

MATT (*having to stop*). No, son . . . I used tae could run up this hill as if there was nae height tae it . . .

JEAN (*taking* MATT*'s arm*). Come on an' we'll walk th' gither . . .

MATT. Walk the old walks . . .

JEAN. It's no' sae far wi' a frien' by your side . . .

MATT. No' sae far an' no sae dark . . . (*Stands straight.*) I'm here noo' . . . I'm standin' here . . . (*Staggers.*)

JEAN. We'll rest if you want . . .

MATT. I'm no' needin' ony rest! (*Pushes her arm away.*) Naw, naw, there's a climb yet . . .

TOMMY. Up an' up . . .

MATT. Aye . . . Tae the tap . . . (*Makes no move.*) Richt tae . . . Tae the . . . (*Stands still.*) Mind they songs, Jean . . . At the school . . . (*Sings.*)

There was a sang
That aye I wad be singin';
There was a star,
An' clear it used tae shine;
An' liltin' in the starlicht
Thro' the shadows
I gaed lang syne . . .

But you never liked tae sing . . .

JEAN (*placing her shawl around his shoulders*). We'll walk
   th'gither . . .

Enter TAM *and* WILLIE, *in their suits from the dance.*
WILLIE *is drunk, leans on* TAM.

WILLIE (*unsteady*). Watch yoursel', Tam, or you'll fa' doon . . .

JEAN. Wha's there?

WILLIE. Naeb'dy worth the kennin' . . .

TOMMY. Came tae us, Tammy Burnet . . . He came tae us . . .

TAM. Jean Cairney . . . Matt?

WILLIE. Is that you, Matt? The great man himsel' . . . The
   Grand Panjandrum . . . I didnae see you at the dance . . .
   No' that you missed much . . . No' what it was . . . Left
   them tae it . . . Is that you, Matt?

TOMMY. Came tae us . . .

WILLIE. Your brother, Matt . . . He's awa wi' his wife . . .
   Drove past me like thunder . . . Foot tae the flair . . . Near
   had me in the ditch . . . He's awa wi' his wife . . . But you'll
   likely ken that . . .

JEAN. Leave him be.

WILLIE. Jean Cairney . . . Is this you fun' yoursel a man?
   You're a wild woman richt enough . . .

TAM. Haud your tongue,Willie! . . . Matt? Do you no' ken us,
   Matt?

MATT. I ken you fine . . . Geordie Burnet . . . I've kent you
   a' my life . . . A guid man . . . I've been wantin' tae say
   that . . . Yin o' the best . . . It's been needin' said . . .

WILLIE. She was at his side . . . Up in the wagon . . . He's
   awa wi' his wife!

TAM. Come on, Willie . . . Hame . . .

JEAN. Thank-you, Tam.

TAM. Goodnicht tae you, Matt . . .

MATT (*beyond answering*). Hame . . . (JEAN *leads* MATT
   away.)

TOMMY. Goodnicht, Tammy Burnet.

TAM. Goodnicht, son . . .

> TOMMY *follows* JEAN *and* MATT *up the hill towards the summit.*

WILLIE. We'll hae flags an' fireworks, will we no'? Flags an' fireworks . . .

TAM. Move yoursel' . . .

WILLIE (*leaning on his knees, giddy with drink*). Did you see the hill this mornin', Tam, wi' the sun catchin' it a clout o' red an' gold . . . Magnificent . . . But noo . . . Noo it's just the hill at the back o' Pollock's Farm, an' the back o' beyond richt enough . . .

TAM. I'll no' wait for you . . .

WILLIE. See doon there . . . Rab's yard . . . It's a guid goin' concern when you see it frae here . . .

TAM. It is that . . .

WILLIE. Would you want it?

TAM. Want it? . . . Naw, I wouldnae want it . . .

WILLIE. Naw, I wouldnae want it neither . . . Come on here, ye clown, till I help you hame . . .

TAM (*Supporting* WILLIE). Aye, Willie . . . Help me hame . . . (TAM *and* WILLIE *go*.)

> JEAN *helps* MATT *down, sits close by him.*

MATT. Jean?

JEAN. I'm here . . .

MATT. Jean Cairney . . .

JEAN. Are you frichtened, Matt?

TOMMY. Sojer . . . Strong . . .

JEAN. I'm here by you . . .

MATT. You were ay that saft an' quiet . . . You thocht that much o' me?

JEAN. I did, aye, an' I dae still . . .

MATT (*in pain*). Jean . . . Jean Cairney . . .

JEAN (*holding him close*). Sssh . . . I'm here . . . I'm here noo' . . . (*Kisses him.*) We've come frae a lang lang way away an' there's a great distance yet tae go . . .

TOMMY. Up an' up . . .

MATT (*afraid*). Intae the dark . . . (*A tremor shakes his body.*)

JEAN. Intae the licht, Matt . . . Intae the licht . . .

MATT. They couldnae dae wi'out me . . . When the big gun got pulled doon in the mire they'd ca' for me by name . . . By name . . . An' me an' the horse would pull it clear th'gither . . .

JEAN (*cradles his head*). Are you fa'in' intae a dream, Matt?

MATT. A dream . . . Is that what it is?

JEAN. Aye . . . Back tae sleep noo' . . . You're hame . . .

MATT. Hame . . .

JEAN. Back tae sleep . . . Be at peace . . . (*He dies.*)

TOMMY. Sojer . . .

JEAN (*sings quietly*).
There was a sang;
But noo, I cannae mind it,
There was a star;
But noo, it disnae shine . . .

TOMMY. Sojer . . . Strong . . .

JEAN (*sings quietly*).
There was a love that led me
Thro' the shadows –
And it *was* mine.

Gie yoursel' ower to the keepin' o' the stars an' the earth . . .

TOMMY. Strong . . .

JEAN. Be at peace . . .

TOMMY *backs away from them, turns struggles to speak.*

TOMMY (*lost, defiant*). Strong . . . Strong!

Fade lights.

End.

3 December 1999 – 8 January 2000
Royal Lyceum Theatre Company
Peter Pan
by J M Barrie
in a version by Stuart Paterson
Matinees at 2.30pm, evenings at 7pm
Tickets: £8 – £15
Children Half Price
Four Family and Friends £38
Main Sponsor
Atlantic TELECOM
Box Office: 0131 248 4848

A Nick Hern Book

King of the Fields first published in Great Britain in 1999
as an original paperback by Nick Hern Books Limited,
14 Larden Road, London W3 7ST, in association with
the Traverse Theatre, Edinburgh

King of the Fields copyright © Stuart Paterson 1999

The author has asserted his moral right to be identified as
the author of this work

Lines from 'There was a Sang' by Helen Cruickshank, from
Scottish Love Poems, edited by Antonia Fraser, published in 1975
by Canongate Books, 14 High Street, Edinburgh EH1,
reproduced with permission

Typeset by Country Setting, Kingsdown, Kent CT14 8ES

Printed and bound in Great Britain by Athenaeum Press,
Gateshead NE11 0PZ

A CIP catalogue record for this book is available from
the British Library

ISBN 1 85459 477 X